Penguin Masterstudies

KU-034-434

The Prologue to The Canterbury Tales

John E. Cunningham was educated at the Lawrence Sheriff School, Rugby, and the University of Birmingham, where, as an undergraduate and later as a research scholar, he studied under the late Professor Allardyce Nicoll. He is the author of books on the Victorian theatre and on Elizabethan and Restoration drama. He has been an Examiner in English for several of the major G.C.E. boards, and is currently Examiner in General Studies for the Oxford and Cambridge Board. He has also lectured for the Workers' Educational Association, written courses for Wolsey Hall, Oxford, and been a tutor at the Open University. He has taught English in both public and maintained schools, and is now Head of the Department of English at Varndean Sixth Form College, Brighton. He was given a complete edition of Chaucer's works in 1943 and is still trying to read it with greater understanding.

Penguin Masterstudies
Advisory Editors:
Stephen Coote and Bryan Loughrey

Chaucer

The Prologue to The Canterbury Tales

John E. Cunningham

Penguin Books

Penguin Books Ltd Harmondsworth, Middlesex, England
Viking Penguin Inc., 40 West 23rd Street, New York, New York 10010, U.S.A.
Penguin Books Australia Ltd, Ringwood, Victoria, Australia
Penguin Books Canada Ltd, 2801 John Street, Markham, Ontario, Canada L3R 1B4
Penguin Books (N.Z.) Ltd 182 190 Wairau Road, Auckland 10, New Zealand

First published 1985

Made and printed in Great Britain by
Richard Clay (The Chaucer Press) Ltd, Bungay, Suffolk
Filmset in 9/11pt Monophoto Times by
Northumberland Press Ltd, Gateshead, Tyne and Wear

Contents

Acknowledgements

Anyone who has been studying and trying to teach an author for forty years will have acquired a mass of information and ideas much of which it is impossible to trace to its sources. It follows that no formal acknowledgements of scholastic debts can be paid, though the Bibliography will give some indication of major sources. The author would like, however, to express his personal thanks to a number of people who have helped him greatly: to two critics, as candid as kindly, Stephen Coote and Bryan Loughrey; to Kenneth Grose, to whom his debts increase as the years pass by; and to his Gode Wyf, without whom this book, like many other things, would never have happened.

J.E.C.

Introduction

Anyone who is about to study a work of literature has to bear in mind two questions. What did this mean when it was written? What does it mean now? To understand the writing of the past we have to know something of the background, the general views which the author and his first readers had, the possible changes there have been not only in the direct meaning but also in the overtones of the words he uses. If what we are studying is truly a work of art, each age will find something new in it, some reflection of itself: Shakespeare would probably be very surprised to see a modern performance of *Hamlet*, just as we should find an eighteenth-century production of it downright funny, and no doubt the twenty-first century will consider the play afresh.

Anyone about to study Chaucer – and *The Prologue* is deservedly the work of his with which most people begin – is likely to ask two other questions. Why should I read this at all? If I must read it to satisfy some syllabus requirement, why can I not read it in a modern version? The purpose of this Introduction is to try to answer these two questions; the purpose of the whole book is to help towards an answer to the first pair – what did it mean and what does it mean?

Chaucer lived from about 1340 to 1400: that is to say, he lived during a period of great and exciting changes, many of which are reflected in the stories he told and the remarkable collection of characters he assembled to tell them. At the beginning of the century in which he was born, the mass of English people worked on the land and lived in villages. Towns were few and very small. Most labourers had strips of land – you can still see the pattern of ridges and furrows in pastureland all over England – which produced enough for them to live on; but they held these from their feudal overlord, and had to give him so many days' free labour on his own estates each year. They were not free to move, or even to marry, without his consent. This is why none of them appear on the pilgrimage to Canterbury. The only 'labourer' is a skilled workman, a ploughman who could sell his services and probably had a little land of his own as well.

The pattern loosely called serfdom suggests a slave state to a modern reader, but the feudal system was not wholly oppressive. True, the Church exacted a tithe or tenth of everyone's income – the state today demands a third of ours in return for varying material provisions for our welfare, and we do not enjoy the 165 holy days or holidays that were in the medieval calendar. In feudal England everyone had reciprocal duties and obligations, though then as always it was easier for those in the higher levels of society to neglect their responsibilities while insisting ruthlessly on their fulfilment by those below them. But this system had creaked along after a fashion since the Norman Conquest. When Chaucer was a small boy it was, as we shall see, suddenly and appallingly disrupted by natural causes. When he was a middle-aged man he lived through another upheaval, this time a social one, which one historian has called 'the most remarkable incident in our long history – the capture of London'. The second event evolved from the first. Both were to affect Chaucer's world profoundly.

The first crisis was the Black Death, which spread throughout England in 1348–9, and remained dormant, with sporadic outbreaks in the summer and occasional very severe recurrences, until the latter part of the seventeenth century. The first outbreak which swept across Europe killed perhaps a third of the population. In the words of a contemporary, 'half the world died', and that is how it must have seemed to them. It is hard to judge the effect on people's minds. Today most of us do not believe in a vengeful God or in Hell: we expect diseases to have ascertainable causes, and to be curable or at least capable of alleviation. If we try to imagine the effects of international nuclear war, we may get some sense of the scale and horror of the Plague, but at least we know how atomic weapons work, what they are, who has them – and can, if we wish, try to prevent such devices being used. Nobody knew how the Black Death was caused or carried. Nobody was safe from it, aristocrat and peasant, priest and murderer, child and adult. It embedded itself deep in the national consciousness of the survivors. Many of Chaucer's stories remind us that death was just round the corner – *The Pardoner's Tale*, *The Monk's Tale* and *The Knight's Tale*, for example; and when he tells us that men feared the Reeve 'like the death', he may have meant 'like the Black Death'. Every year it returned to remind folk of their frail grip on this mortal world.

Besides this spiritual effect, which must have made many people look with a more critical eye at the Church, as Chaucer certainly does in his *Prologue*, there was an enormous social result. Suddenly there was a serious shortage of labour to work feudal property. Men realized that they could escape from their villages and seek someone who would pay them wages for their services. So began, for many working men, the mobility of labour which was to give labourers themselves an inkling of their own power and importance. The second upheaval referred to took place in 1381. In the south-eastern part of England, a group of labourers who had been subjected to some very unpopular taxation gathered together, marched on London, took the Tower, executed the Archbishop of Canterbury, murdered foreign workmen such as Flemish weavers and were pacified only by the courage – and duplicity – of the teenage king, Richard II, who promised to meet their demands.

Thus twice in his life Chaucer must have felt he had seen the world turned upside down. Though there are few direct references to these events in his writing, nevertheless we can trace an awareness of change and instability, an interest in classes that were vanishing, like the Knight, and in the rising men of the middle classes, merchants and skilled tradesmen.

Above all, the pilgrimage itself is a sign of people's need for a faith in troubled times – the assembly at the Tabard are going to Canterbury to pay their dues to the martyr who had helped them 'when they were sick', a term which covers both bodily and mental states. Scholars have sometimes tried to set a date for the pilgrimage, as though it were a real event. This is an amusing but unimportant game to play. However, the sort of date arrived at by studying internal evidence, such as the Knight's campaigns, suggests only a few years after the Peasants' Revolt took place.

The upheavals we have mentioned were internal. The background to the whole of Chaucer's life, rarely mentioned perhaps because it was always there, was the Hundred Years War. This long dynastic struggle for power in France began a few years before Chaucer was born and continued until half a century after his death. For much of his lifetime England was under an unstable government because Edward III outlived his own eldest son, the Black Prince, whose tomb is still one of the glories of Canterbury, thus leaving a little grandson as nominal ruler of the country. That grandson, Richard II, was to gather round him a court of high fashion, much of it based on French models, and his country was the harder to rule – because the earlier successes in the French wars had brought prosperity, not to say loot, to campaigners good and bad, and the prosperity of local men tends to increase national violence and unrest. Something of the turbulent state of the realm may be found in one of Chaucer's most vivid pieces of writing, the description of the Temple of Mars in *The Knight's Tale*. As a youth, Chaucer had served abroad like the Knight and seen the world of action at first hand.

At home, one other result of the war was the presence of a number of French aristocratic prisoners, some of whom had to wait years for their ransoms to be paid, and who led quite relaxed lives, encouraging foreign graces, clothes, cookery, styles of courtship, all of which are reflected in *The Tales*. Yet with regard to their language, another most important change was taking place as Chaucer grew up. Latin was, and remained until the eighteenth century, an international language for men of learning, and most serious works were written in it. When the Normans conquered England, their new subjects spoke various dialects of Old English or Anglo-Saxon – a strong, gritty, Germanic tongue with a very complex grammar. The Normans – who were Viking settlers in France, as their name, North-men, shows – brought their own brand of French with them to this country, and this continued to be the language of the court and of officialdom until Chaucer's day, though it underwent modifications and became less like the French spoken in France. The 'English' population naturally picked up words from their masters, and soon many people who had to deal between the classes would have been bilingual. The complex grammar of Old English began to be simplified, its vocabulary extended, so that in Chaucer's lifetime two significant acts of recognition took place: English, rather than French, became the official language in which lawsuits were pleaded; and it also became the recognized language of instruction in schools. There is some argument about which English king was the first to speak English as his native language, but Richard II certainly spoke it, and his successor, Henry IV, who ruled in the last year of Chaucer's life, seems to have made it his language of choice.

Chaucer's friend and contemporary Gower wrote works in English, French and Latin, and Chaucer was quite capable of doing this too – probably he could have managed Italian as well – but it is of great significance that he chose to write his very wide range of works, his technical treatise on astronomy, his long novel in verse, his prose version of a famous philosopher, occasional poems, courtly romances and the immense diversity of *The Canterbury Tales*, in his own English. We can call it 'his own' because he used a dialect form, that of the East Midlands. This, which tended to become the accepted speech of the capital, was to help the movement towards the idea of a standardized form of English, a problem which was brought to a head in the next century by the introduction of printing. (We should remember that Chaucer's work, like almost all medieval literature, was to be read aloud to an audience from a single, expensive manuscript.) In a famous preface Caxton tells us a story of how in one part of England the plural of 'egg' was 'eyren', in another part 'eggs'. If he was to print books for wide circulation, which form was he to choose?

It may have occurred to some readers by now to think that Chaucer lived in times not unlike our own. The present century has seen enormous change in social structure, upheavals in conditions of labour, political unrest at home and a constant background of wars and fear of wars abroad. Our language, too, has changed: there has been a vast influx of new words coined to meet our technological innovations, so much so that Chambers find it necessary to publish a separate dictionary to contain them. The mention of dictionaries may remind us of another kind of standardization that Chaucer never imagined or cared about – the idea of 'correct' spelling. The spread of radio and television means that we now have a concept of a 'correct' way of pronouncing our language, though luckily these same media also help to keep local accents alive; but an accent is not a dialect, and few genuine dialect-speakers remain.

So, in a way, Chaucer's experience of the world may have had some similarities with ours; but there are also very great differences, and we must consider some of these if we are to make sense of the group of people he presents to us in *The Prologue*.

Indeed, we might begin with the following activity. People still go on pilgrimages, but they are not popular in this country. Chaucer's world was a Roman Catholic world, and he believed in Heaven, Hell and Purgatory. Over the chancel arch of many country churches we can still see the remains of the lurid painting of the Last Judgement which was there to remind the simple worshipper every Sunday of what was in store for him. The Church pervaded every corner of life, where now it is at best peripheral and to many people wholly irrelevant. When we come to look at the pilgrims, we shall see what a large number of them were in some way connected with the Church. The monasteries still sometimes fulfilled their functions of tending the needy and encouraging study, but many were wealthy and idle. If the local priest could barely patter through the Latin of the Mass, there were wandering preachers, friars and pardoners amongst them, who could entertain with a rousing sermon – a reminder that an illiterate population enjoyed the act of listening in a way hard for us to conceive of. Where books were rare and very costly, and writing materials were hard to come by and to use, people relied on an accurate verbal memory far more than we do.

Yet about many things they might seem extremely vague. If you had asked Chaucer what date it was or what time it was or how old he was or how he wrote his own name, he would probably have been surprised at the question and given surprising answers. He thought of dates in terms of the Church festivals and the calendar of astrology; time he might think of in terms of the seven offices of the religious day, the so-called 'canonical hours', and each monastery kept its own. And there were two quite separate systems of measuring time: one was based on our notion of the twenty-four-hour day, the other on the division of the day from sunrise to sunset and then again to sunrise into two groups of twelve, so that, except at the equinoxes, the hours were never of the same length in daylight that they were in darkness. The time-scheme of *The Tales*, both in regard to dates and to times of day, is very vague to us, but would have been quite adequate when written. He wrote his own name as he pleased, and if he tended to keep to one spelling it was perhaps because it was easy to write or looked attractive. It is on record that on one occasion, when required to give his age, he said that he was 'over forty', and that was probably about how he thought of it. The date of his birth would never have been recorded in any official way – only of his baptism. A keen astronomer-astrologer (to him there was no difference), he was sure that the planets, all *seven* of them as he thought, revolved around the Earth, which was the centre of the Universe since it contained God's greatest creation. The social hierarchy of the day may have been crumbling, as we have seen, but its distinctions were quite clear to him. The famous question 'Who does he think he is?' could hardly have been asked in the fourteenth century, for it would have had no meaning. Everyone knew who he was in the social order, though of course some aspired to better themselves. On the whole, however, Chaucer would not expect the future, if he thought about it, to exhibit very much change; the past – which he wrote about a great deal – he would not have seen as very different from the present. Since he believed that people did not change in any fundamental way, he did not trouble himself with historical perspective, and wrote about the past – as Shakespeare was to do in his Roman plays – much as if it were the present.

We, however, have been approaching him from rather different assumptions, and perhaps we have now gone far enough, in this short introduction, to be able to consider again the two questions we posed at the beginning: why should we read him, and why read him in the original language?

If we have any interest in the language and literature of our country at all, we must read some Chaucer. He lived at a time which was vital to the development of both. English – still different in many ways, as we shall see, from our own, but recognizably English – was developing quickly, both as a language and as an accepted means of expression and thought and record on a wide variety of topics. The form of English in which he wrote was to set the pattern for the form of English which was to become standard. His proficiency in other languages has been mentioned: as we shall see later, he used the techniques of French and Italian in the way in which he constructed his poetry, rather than the quite different systems used in Old English, and he was the first major writer to combine the English language with European forms of stanza and metre.

As we have seen, the times he lived in bear some comparison to our own. One of the great differences we have noted is that most enjoyment of literature was aural. The soul of poetry is its sound, together with the associations which words carry with them beyond their mere definitions. We cannot hope to understand this remarkable author fully, or to enjoy him, unless we can get at the sense that his words conveyed to his hearers, so we must study his language; and, though this is more difficult, it is possible also to learn how to 'hear' him as we read, to hear the extraordinary and powerful mixture of sounds that emerge from the welding together of two languages that were of such different origin. How we may do this will be dealt with later. A bland, modern translation may be pleasant to read, but will never do more than give us the general sense of what he wrote. Our bland, modern pronunciation takes all the grit and guts out of the language – can you imagine someone telling a Scottish or Irish joke in a standard English accent?

One writer, perhaps over-fond of turning a good phrase, said that Chaucer 'invented the English language'. This is not a wholly extravagant claim, since his influence on it has been enormous. If we are to begin to study what we like to call our heritage, this is as good a place to start as we could find. *The Prologue*, with its vivid gallery of medieval people, makes an appropriate gateway through which we may follow his other readers, adapters, translators and admirers, of whom Shakespeare, Dryden and Scott are but a few of the diverse throng.

1. Chaucer's Life

For the convenience of someone coming to Chaucer's work for the first time, we give here a simple account of some of the main facts of his life, together with a comment on aspects which are of particular relevance in studying his writing. Much fuller treatments of his life are, of course, available for those who wish to pursue this further. (Suggestions are made in the Bibliography.)

Chaucer was born about 1340. His father and grandfather were both Londoners, though the latter came from Ipswich. His father, John Chaucer, was a citizen, a term which then carried some connotations of status, and dealt in wine. At the time of the poet's birth, he had a connection with the court of Edward III, so it was not too difficult for him to obtain a place there for his son, as a page to the wife of the Duke of Clarence.

At nineteen, Chaucer was serving abroad in the royal forces in France as a squire, was captured and ransomed by the king himself. About eight years later, in 1369, he was granted a life-pension by the king in recognition of his services in the royal household. This pension was for a little more than thirteen pounds a year. It is impossible even to suggest a modern equivalent, but it has been said that a country parson at that time would consider he had quite a comfortable little living if his annual income was ten pounds. One of his first poems of any substance was a reflection of his royal connections. In an outbreak of plague in 1369, the first wife of John of Gaunt, Duke of Lancaster, died, and Chaucer composed a work in her memory, *The Book of the Duchess*. Lionel, Duke of Clarence, had died the previous year, and Chaucer's services seem to have been largely transferred to Gaunt. In the next few years he was certainly busy at court, and he also engaged in some diplomatic activity. Perhaps the most important aspect of this, for us, is his being sent, at the end of 1372, on a mission to Italy, where he remained for the best part of a year. He apparently fulfilled his official tasks well, because from the time of his return he prospered. He was given an important office in the Port of London, a daily ration of wine, a life-pension from Gaunt, and took a lease of a house in Aldgate. His ties with the Lancastrian house were probably increased by his marriage to Philippa, since there is reason to believe that she was sister to the lady who became Gaunt's mistress and, later, his third wife.

The pattern of the next few years is one of steady prosperity and favour. He received a number of gifts and offices, went to Flanders in 1377 on a secret mission, to France and Italy again the following year, and was given an additional post in the Customs in 1382. Three years later, possibly again through royal favour, he was allowed to hold his offices but appoint someone else to carry them out – given, in fact, a sinecure. In 1386 he was appointed Knight of the Shire for Kent – that is, he represented Kent in the Commons when Parliament was summoned.

Perhaps this marked the zenith of his fortunes. We have noted elsewhere that he lived in a troubled century, and there was a constant battle for power amongst the surviving sons of Edward III, which his young grandson, Richard II, had great difficulty in controlling. It was in one of the abrupt shifts of influence, when Gaunt was out of the country – he left for Spain in the summer of 1386 – that Chaucer fell from favour. He lost his official offices, and was in such straits that he had to raise money on his pensions, rather as we now raise cash on insurance policies. His wife died the following year; but there was an ironic twist in store in 1389, when a new shift of power brought John of Gaunt back into prominence, and Chaucer was appointed Clerk of the King's Works at a salary of nearly forty pounds a year, an important position as it entailed responsibility for royal buildings. To this post was added, the following year, the appointment to a similar responsibility at St George's Chapel, Windsor, and he had a number of commissions related to this. However, life continued to be erratic: he gave up his chief post in 1391, perhaps because he had suffered robbery and assault while carrying out duties which were now harder in view of his age, and became sole forester of North Petherton Park in 1398, another sinecure. There are indications, hard to analyse, that he may have been short of money, and he was sued for a modest debt at this time.

The year 1399 was an important one for England, as in it the king's cousin, Henry of Bolingbroke, took the throne from Richard. This was to be the beginning of a long struggle for power between the houses of York and Lancaster and caused several uprisings, since Henry IV, the title he took, was not in line for the throne, being the son of a younger son. Richard died childless, and the Duke of Clarence, to whose issue the crown should have gone, left no male heir. This struggle took nearly a century to be resolved, until the accession of Henry Tudor as Henry VII after the Battle of Bosworth, in 1485, ended the Wars of the Roses.

Chaucer was concerned with more immediate problems. He wrote a poem to the new king lamenting the state of his own purse, and Henry granted him a good pension, which may have encouraged him to take a long lease on a house in Westminster. This was optimistic for a man of his years in those times. He died the following year, and is buried in the Abbey. Of his family not much is known for certain. He had a son – 'little Lewis' he calls him in the book he wrote explaining the use of the astrolabe, an astronomical instrument, to the boy, but he seems to have died young. If the direct line died with him, we need not be surprised. Such extinction was common enough. Until the medical advances of the late nineteenth century, people had little power to cure illnesses which are now regarded as trivial but were formerly often fatal.

All this is mostly facts and figures, and different commentators have put quite different interpretations upon them. For example, Chaucer has been seen as a middle-class boy who made good, as the product of royal patronage, as a good civil servant, as a 'European' (an expression he would not have understood), as an opportunist and, for other reasons, as an unhappily married man. It is worth spending a few moments looking at some of these assertions to see whether they have any validity, and also whether they help us to understand his poetry.

The assumption that he was unhappily married is based upon the silliest of evidence – he makes almost no references to his wife that have survived, and in his stories he tells a number of tales of unfaithful women. If a man is happily married, he is not always referring to the fact, and probably feels more keenly for those who do not share his fortune, so the 'evidence' can be used to prove the contrary at our pleasure. As for patronage, it was the usual way to get on in the world then, and remained so until at least the beginning of the present century. He was fortunate in having more than one connection with the court. He was obviously a man who could be trusted, being sent abroad several times on diplomatic missions, and he had served as a page in a royal retinue and as a young soldier, besides the more dignified offices of his mature years.

What is clear from this picture is that he had seen a lot of life – aristocratic, bureaucratic, military, diplomatic. In his travels and his various duties, he had had to brush shoulders with many different kinds of people, and he was an observant man. Luckily, however we interpret his own success, it did not make him a snob, and in his writing he looks upon people of almost every rank with an impartial eye – social snobbery he found amusing, and gently satirizes it in his picture of the aristocratic Prioress. As to his being a 'European' – a term which did not then exist in our sense, for he divided the world simply into Christian and heathen – he had a good knowledge of French and French culture from the English court before he went to its country of origin. His visit to Italy certainly impressed him: there he made himself acquainted with the work of

Boccaccio and probably Dante, who, just like Chaucer, had taken the major step of deciding to write a major, serious poem in his own ordinary language, not in Latin. But a fluent command of a couple of languages does not make a man a cosmopolitan, and there were vast reaches of Europe quite unknown to him – in one way he seemed to have a rather parochial mind, for he regarded a large part of his own country as being wild and strange. His Shipman comes from the West Country, and Chaucer says of him, 'For all I know he came from Dartmouth', rather as we might say, 'He's South American – maybe Bolivian', and he speaks of the north as though it were a territory of unknown barbarism, an attitude not wholly unknown in the south-east to this day. Possibly he himself found this amusing in his fellow-Londoners, for he may have visited the northern estates of his royal master as a young man, and he knew and used the wit and dialect of the north to good effect in *The Reeve's Tale*.

Undeniably, his travels affected his work. Though he chose to write in English, he did so in the metres and verse-patterns of France and Italy. If all his pilgrims are English, they often tell stories set in other countries, and he shows local knowledge of Brittany in *The Franklin's Tale* and of Italy in *The Clerk's Tale*.

This is a suitable moment to remind ourselves that, though he is best known for *The Canterbury Tales*, he was a man of astonishing output: astonishing, that is, if we consider how busy he was in worldly affairs and how slow the process of writing was, even if it were dictated. Not only the bulk of his work, but its range must impress us. He translated a courtly allegory, the *Romaunt of the Rose*, and a long philosophical work, the former from French, the latter from Latin; he wrote what many people would call the first English novel, the story of Troilus and Cressida, told in a highly elaborate and tricky verse-form. He wrote a handbook on the use of the astrolabe for his eleven-year-old son – an extremely difficult thing to do in the laboured prose of the time, which was quite unsuited to technical writing. He also wrote a number of short poems, some of them very fine, which give us insights into his own feelings and experience.

If there is indeed a key to unlock a man's life, in Chaucer's case it might be found in one of the translations referred to above. Boethius' *Consolation of Philosophy* was written by a sixth-century Italian while he was in prison awaiting death. It deals with the ups and downs of life, and with ways of coping with triumph and disaster. Chaucer's life exhibits a pattern of good times and bad, sometimes with quite sudden changes, always, it seems, depending upon the good will or caprice of others more powerful than he. He had, we can surely say with confidence, a good understanding of the transitory nature of our changeable world, and the image of the Wheel of Fortune – 'Now up, now down, as bucket in a well' – that is central to the first of the tales is no mere rhetorical figure to him. He well knew that life is lived – or was, in his time – in a perpetual state of unstable equilibrium, and this he learned to accept with quiet humility. Our own age is so conscious of its technical achievement that it tends to regard mortality itself as something for which there ought to be a cure, and finding it is only a matter of time. In this man's modest life we might find a lesson in modesty.

2. The Framework of the Tales

It is in *The Prologue* that the framework of the whole of *The Canterbury Tales* is set up, in two ways: the number of stories to be told and the manner of their telling; and, perhaps more important, the cast that is to recount these stories is introduced. In studying *The Prologue*, then, we should have some idea of what these characters were about to do.

Chaucer's intention was to produce a comprehensive anthology of contemporary stories of a very wide range. The problem faced by anyone compiling such a collection is to make them cohere, to find some way which will form a unity of diversity. As we have mentioned, he knew – and borrowed from – the work of Boccaccio, and many English readers will know Boccaccio's collection of a hundred stories known as *The Decameron*, if only for its somewhat saucy reputation. Boccaccio's means of stringing these together is simple, plausible and ingenious: ten young Italian aristocrats, men and women, take a villa in the country while there is an outbreak of plague in Florence. To while away the days, they suggest that each day they appoint a Master or Mistress of Ceremonies, who will give them a theme, and then each will tell a story based upon it. After ten days, the plague abates, and they return, so rounding off the book. The author is able in this way to introduce ten groups of tales, each centred on a particular theme, with a little linking commentary about the re-actions to each story when it is done. Yet reading this work is quite unlike reading Chaucer, and the reason is not far to seek. All these story-tellers are of the same age and class, and, but for their names, might be of the same sex too. They all talk at the same level and in much the same urbane style, whatever the topic. Chaucer hit upon a much more flexible device. One of the few occasions in his day when a great variety of people rubbed shoulders with one another, and talked and enjoyed themselves and told stories, was on pilgrimages. Only the social extremes – royalty rode with its own retinue, serfs could not leave their land – would be missing, though there would not be many women in such parties. The idea of the pilgrim-age, then, is an excellent one for providing a social mixture. It may be argued that he had a further, symbolic, purpose which was to be part of the whole design – these people are riding from the world of men, the pub in Southwark, to the city of God, the great shrine at Canterbury. There is some evidence, as we shall see, that he had this at the back of his mind, but it must be pointed out at once that people went on pilgrimages for many different reasons, just as today some folk on a charter flight to Athens may be archaeologists, others Greek scholars, others sun-seekers, others going to visit friends and so on. Quite a few of the pilgrims were there on business – the Pardoner, for instance, hoped to make money on the way – and some just enjoyed company and travel, like the Wife of Bath. Moreover, the design was not to end in Canterbury, but back in Southwark.

The pattern is proposed by the Host of the Tabard Inn. He proposes it as a way of ensuring further custom. Chaucer says there were fully twenty-nine people there – though by what arithmetic he reached this underestimate is not clear – and on the road they are joined by the Canon's Yeoman. The Host suggests that all of them tell two stories on the way to Canterbury and two more on the way back, and the teller judged to be best is to have a feast at the expense of the rest of them – in the Host's inn, of course. He offers to ride with them and act as referee, and imposes the condition that anyone who rebels against his ruling is to pay all their travelling expenses. It is hard to resist the speculation that Chaucer intended this to happen, but, as we all know, he came nowhere near to completing the work, which would have entailed approximately 120 stories.

What he did manage to do was block out some sections of the whole, including the beginning and the end, and several other parts can be seen to be in sequence because he provides connecting material. The first story is told, correctly, by the man of highest rank, the Knight, who draws the first lot. It is a tale of chivalry and earthly love of a very refined and noble kind. The last story – we know it is the last, because Chaucer wrote a special kind of epilogue to it – is told by one of the humblest people present, the poor country Parson, brother to the Ploughman, and it is a sermon. Few people read it nowadays, but it has a good deal of interest. It deals with the seven deadly sins, those, that is, that kill our hopes of immortal life for ever by condemning us to Hell; and it also offers remedies for all these sins, ways of trying to avoid or atone for them. So perhaps Chaucer did, after all, have some overriding concept of a story of a pilgrimage which begins with a secular love-story – though told by a pious man – and ends with a statement of faith. Certainly one of his major themes is love: medieval thinkers were able to make a very clear distinction in Latin between *caritas* and *cupiditas*, which the modern words 'charity' and 'cupidity' do not well convey. By the latter was meant the sort of love which asks for something – love of money, power, of another person from whom you expect to have pleasure; by the former was meant that love which St Paul speaks of in a famous passage in

Corinthians, the love that gives and asks nothing back, the love of God which we are urged to try, as best we may, to emulate. Many of the tales do indeed deal with love, both sacred and profane; and with associated ideas, such as duty to God and Man; with the abuse of that love, its blasphemous or absurd other face; and with 'gentilesse', that word we cannot translate, which means the whole concept of the duty of the strong towards the weak. With such a variety of story-tellers at his command, Chaucer could explore many facets of this greatest of subjects. It is time to look at the way in which the characters who are to tell the tales are presented.

It is here that we run headlong into a thicket bristling with thorns, and no academic analysis can do more than suggest how thorny it is. There are several ways of looking at the characters who make up the band of pilgrims. The most popular is to divide them into three: the characters who are merely mentioned, like the three Nuns or the Guildsmen, with virtually no attempt to describe them at all; those that are supposed to be 'types', formal portraits of a class or craft or profession, such as the Shipman; and those that are three-dimensional and come completely to life, like the Wife of Bath. An extension of the last group is the notion that some of the pilgrims are based on people whom Chaucer actually knew.

As a working hypothesis, this division is fair enough, and you may find that it is quite adequate for your purposes. First, however, we should be quite sure that what we call 'character' and what Chaucer called 'complexion' mean the same thing. He believed, as people had believed since the fourth century BC, that human beings had four fluids inside them, the mixture ('complexion') of which, taken in conjunction with the position of the planets at the time of their birth, determined their character, behaviour and appearance. We still use words – sanguine, phlegmatic, choleric and melancholy – to denote four temperaments, and we would still probably think of a melancholy person as pale, a choleric person as high-coloured. Chaucer believed, in common with other educated people of the time, that these characteristics were respectively the product of an excess of blood (*sang* in French), phlegm, choler, and black choler or bile. The idea is not as silly as it sounds. We believe, after all, that a person's character is partly the product of their body chemistry, of the genetic DNA coding and of the balance of the glands, such as the thyroid, which, if upset, can produce changes in behaviour and temperament – indeed, in their very appearance.

Not only did Chaucer have a slightly different view of 'character' from our own, tending simply to put mankind into four types (if you have read

Hamlet it might strike you at this point that Shakespeare thought in the same way: the four young men, Hamlet, Laertes, Horatio and Fortinbras are, respectively, melancholy, choleric, phlegmatic and sanguine); but also, in addition to this basic difference, in the subject called 'rhetoric' which every educated man studied in those days, and which really means the effective use of language, he had learned a stock way of *describing* character. This was largely a matter of describing appearance and demeanour, with no attempt at investigating the psychology of the subject.

One example will suffice to show us how difficult it is to reach clear opinions on this – and, incidentally, may save us time when we come to the detailed commentary on *The Prologue* which is the heart of this little book: the very first pilgrim, the Knight.

The following positions are all tenable. First, he is an idealized portrait of what a knight should have been, but probably no longer was. Certainly he is presented as old-fashioned by comparison with his very fashionable son, who is also brave but has a host of courtly accomplishments his father lacks. So he may be a 'type' of old-fashioned chivalry. Second, he may be based on someone his creator had known, and names have been advanced for this honour. We cannot argue this one, since we do not know what these men were like. A third view is to ignore the dated quality of the account and see him simply as a stereotype of chivalry, valid, with minor adjustments, in any age. A fourth, recently given a good deal of publicity, is that the picture is satirical: the Knight is nothing but an aristocratic freebooter, most of the campaigns he went on were the hunting-ground of the 'free companies' who, having no business in life but war, went and fought wherever there was sport or profit, and all the praise of his good qualities is ironic. The position is extreme, but it has some support if we examine the list of places where he fought. By way of comparison, if we examine the campaigns of Richard I, still popularly called Lionheart, they do not make attractive reading. Add to this that Richard was probably homosexual, and we have excellent material for that most popular of modern pastimes, debunking. To debunk the Knight, who is imaginary, is even easier than to debunk Richard, who really existed.

The answer to the last interpretation, we suggest, lies in taking the character of the Knight in conjunction with the long and elaborate tale he tells. This is, surely, a serious picture of chivalry as it might be, and the charge of satire fails. But whether Chaucer meant the portrayal as a sad reflection of how things had gone to the dogs, or whether it was a tribute to someone he had admired, we simply cannot say, though some critics are not over-shy in proclaiming the truth of their own view.

Similarly, we can only guess at the overall construction of *The Tales*. Yet it is clear that this was to be very carefully worked out. The Knight tells the first story, which is appropriate to his rank – there is a hint that the Host fixed the draw so that he would be the opener – and he should have been followed by someone else of high position. The Host does, in fact, invite the Monk, who is obviously wealthy and worldly, to take up the next place – but Chaucer, good artist that he was, knew that an audience would want a change after a long, highly refined tale of courtly adventure, so the drunken Miller interrupts and will not be silenced. In turn, as he has told a story mocking a carpenter, the only carpenter present – for so the Reeve was trained – retaliates with a scandalous story of a miller. If he had managed his 120 tales, we may be sure Chaucer would have exercised great care in their ordering.

A great deal of scholarship has certainly been expended on trying to work out the overall pattern that was in his mind, including some ingenious theories that groups of the tales deal with specific topics, those which examine the married state being amongst the more notable. It is good for us to remember how much we are indebted to, or at the mercy of, editors of Chaucer for our overall view of him.

Chaucer began *The Tales* about a hundred years before Caxton printed the first books in English. He wrote them, we suppose, for the amusement of his aristocratic patrons. The manuscript of any substantial work of this kind would be copied out by a professional writer, a 'scrivener' as he was called, so that a fair copy could be given to the patron. It is a testimony to Chaucer's popularity that over twenty-five fairly complete manuscripts of *The Tales* survive. It is a testimony to the extensive work of the late Walter Skeat that the edition he published first in 1912 is still accepted as giving the most likely order of the fragments of the whole work. Later editors have adopted different readings of different lines, and spelling varies widely from one text to another – something Chaucer would not have bothered about at all – but Skeat's framework still stands for most readers. The nine groups of stories which he set in order include the first and the last. There is no doubt about the earliest group, since the Knight draws the first lot to determine who shall open, and after that we have a series of linking passages which tell us what is to come next; several of the intermediate groups are similarly linked by comments made by the Host, or arguments amongst the pilgrims about what is to follow; and we know that the last story of all was to be told by the Parson, for his sermon

25

is immediately followed by Chaucer's own conclusion, in which he asks, amongst other things, to be forgiven for those stories which 'tend to be sinful'. He ends by begging mercy of his Maker, to whom he commends his soul. Reading these simple, unaffected lines, we might spare a thought for those patient scholars who have toiled so long to give us a text that we can read coherently.

3. How to Read Chaucer

Most users of this book will be working under professional guidance and instruction: there is no substitute for personal contact in study, where any difficulty or obscurity can be referred directly to the teacher, and any error in one's own understanding will be noticed and corrected. No collection of notes, however exhaustive, can hope to cover all the problems of every student. On the other hand, there is no substitute for working at a text on your own, trying to reach your own understanding and interpretation. Some students, of course, will be working entirely on their own, and are likely to look for all the help they can get. This short chapter attempts to offer suggestions of a fairly fundamental kind which may help those who are working by themselves, whether they are completely on their own or doing so as part of a guided course.

The first question many students ask about Chaucer is: 'Should I buy a crib?' The answer is that a crib, in the sense of a version that solves all the problems, does not exist. There are, however, a variety of versions of Chaucer in more or less contemporary English, both in prose and in verse. An old favourite is the verse 'translation' by Nevill Coghill, which has been enjoyed by many generations of students. This is inexpensive and has two other virtues. It is lively reading and it is uncluttered by a mass of notes. If you want to get a rough *impression* of any of *The Canterbury Tales*, you might find this worth considering. It will enable you to read a number of the stories quickly and easily as a background to *The Prologue*. But can you use it as a 'translation'?

We said that there is no crib to Chaucer. The word is a little old-fashioned, probably because it was most familiar to those of an earlier generation who were brought up to study Latin and Greek. It is possible to get a useful English translation of, say, Livy if you are struggling with the historian's Latin. Latin is a dead language. Its meaning therefore does not change, and once we have found an acceptable equivalent in English for a Latin word we can understand what the author is saying when he uses it. English is a living language. It changes all the time and at certain periods does so very quickly: it was developing very fast when Chaucer wrote – he helped it along – and in Shakespeare's day; it is changing quite a lot today. So to 'translate' Chaucer's own shifting tongue into our shifting tongue is an impossibility, though the attempt can be a challenge and an enjoyment. In the end we have to acquire a feeling for his use of words, just as, however much French we learn, we cannot be at home in the language until we have spent a lot of time amongst people who speak nothing else, and we begin to sense rhythm and idioms and overtones as well as knowing when to use the subjunctive.

We can attempt to achieve this with Chaucer in two ways. The first is by looking systematically at some of the basic difficulties of meaning; the second is by trying to learn something about how his verse originally sounded.

A complete beginner may think his greatest difficulty is to understand a single word of what lies before him! Looking for a moment at the first two lines, however, and reading (you may have a slightly different spelling here and there)

> Whan that Aprille with his shoures sote
> The droghte of Marche hath perced to the rote

it is easy to recognize the month of April, the first word is obviously 'when' and we all know that April brings showers. Probably a helpful footnote will leap to our eye to tell us that 'sote' means 'sweet' or something similar, and if we have a little French we will know that in that language an adjective goes after its noun rather than before, so we cheerfully begin translating, as we think: 'When that April, with his sweet showers, has pierced the drought of March to the root', and so on. This is the approximate sense, but it is in a language that never was on land or sea. Chaucer wrote in a language that was essentially alive – we tend to forget that every author is in fact a 'modern' author in that, when he wrote, his work was up to date, with the rare exception of deliberate imitations of earlier styles. If we are going to try the impossible, to 'translate', we must produce something that is true modern spoken English, colloquial where the original is, formal where it is formal. Editions still current are often very unhelpful in this respect – one widely used is plastered with such unrealistic or unusual words as 'scurrility', 'wanton', 'psaltery', 'baldric' and a host of others, which some students would probably have to look up in a dictionary, which no modern English speaker is likely to use naturally in speech, and which in writing would sound rather ornate or affected in most contexts. Many editions contain notes written by academics who seem to have little idea of how to address anyone who has not graduated in English, so the language problem is made even greater where it should have been lessened.

Let us look at a single line – a very famous one – and see if we can see what difficulties it presents. The first character described is the Knight, and Chaucer says of him (l. 72):

He was a verray parfit gentil knight.

This appears to go straight into modern English – he was a very perfect, gentle knight. It is often so quoted of someone who exhibits what are thought to be the finer qualities of courtesy and so on. It will pass – but it is probably not what Chaucer meant. We have said that words change their sense. In Chaucer we will often find it helpful to consider the root of a word, the meaning it had in the language from which it came (and here a good dictionary is most helpful). 'Perfect' originally meant 'complete', 'finished'. The word here could well mean that he was completely accomplished in the skills appropriate to his calling and position – or it could mean that he was physically a well-made man, though that seems more remote. The word 'gentle' defies any simple modernization. Its first meaning is 'of noble breeding', but by Chaucer's time it carried overtones of courtesy and courage. We shall probably not be too far out if we say, 'He was a thoroughly accomplished, well-bred knight', though even here 'well-bred' sounds a little stiff and dated. But the line has revealed what many students find to be the greatest difficulty of all – words still in use, apparently quite familiar, asking nothing more than to be modernized in their spelling. It is easy to spot the supposedly difficult words, words which have vanished from the language but were common enough in Chaucer's day – 'wight', 'y-clept', 'fetisly', to cite three that appear often – and easy to look up in a glossary and remember them; it is harder to spot the words that remain but in a different sense – hardest of all, perhaps, to discover those which have changed only slightly. A good example of this is the common verb 'can, could', which often has to be translated not simply as 'can' but 'to be able to' or almost 'to know how to', which is the sense that 'can' still carries in 'Can you play chess?'

So far, then, we have established that any version we try to make of Chaucer must be in an English that sounds like the language we actually speak; that we must never take simple words for granted, but check them in a good glossary; and that it is often a great help to try to find the original meaning of a word, or what it would mean to a Frenchman.

Most editions of Chaucer include some notes on his grammar, and some give very extensive ones. You may well have looked at something of the kind in horror, and hastily turned elsewhere. Unless you are going to study the whole development of our language from Old English onwards, it is useless to worry about grammatical structure, which, in any case, was becoming very fluid and irregular in Chaucer's own time. There are certain grammatical signposts which you can learn to spot quite easily, and the most important ones are mentioned as they arise in the detailed commentary on the text which follows. A single example of a useful signpost is given here. We show what grammarians call the past participle by adding '-ed' to the end of a word: thus 'called' is a past tense – 'he has called' and so on. If you have studied German, you will know that in that language something is put at the *beginning* of the word – the prefix 'ge-'. Chaucer here shows the Old English side of his language by using a Germanic form. If you see a word beginning with 'y-', such as 'y-clept', you will soon learn to take it as a past participle: this one means, in fact, 'called' or 'named', and is quite common. You will probably find it is easier to absorb such things as you proceed in your study of the text than to sit down and try to learn a mass of tables of grammatical endings.

Understanding of structure is often easier if we can hear a line spoken, and this leads us to consider how we can learn to 'hear' Chaucer. Most students are probably aware that pronunciation has changed a great deal since he wrote, and again some editions will have long lists of vowels and consonants which are supposed to help us to pronounce Chaucer correctly. These are not, in general, very useful to the average learner.

There are two related problems here. You can never enjoy a poem properly unless you can say it or hear someone else do so, since poetry depends on sound as much as, if not more than, literal meaning. So we have to try to learn not only how Chaucer pronounced his words, but how he spoke lines of verse – what is usually called 'scansion'. Chaucer wrote in English but used a continental system. His poetry is metrical – that is, each line is made up of a number of similar groups of sounds. If you try to say 'Pelicans frequently suffer from belly-ache', you will probably find that you are automatically speaking in a kind of jingle. The line breaks up into four little packets of sound, each one starting with a heavily stressed syllable followed by two lighter ones. The effect of this particular metre is mildly comical. *The Prologue* is written in the metre which was to become the most widely used in English, the metre of Shakespeare's plays and of Milton's great poems, the metre which adapts itself most easily to the rhythms of ordinary speech. The opening of Gray's 'Elegy' will do to show it at its clearest:

Thĕ cúrfĕw tólls thĕ knéll ŏf pártĭng dáy ...

It is easy to see that this consists basically of five groups of sounds, each beginning with a weak stress to be followed by a stronger one. The strong stresses are not all absolutely the same in weight – otherwise the line would be a mere jingle – but they are there, a quiet undercurrent of music to give shape to the line. As in Chaucer's day many words had a lightly stressed sound at the end, his version of this metre is likely to have an extra syllable

– just as in French. The secret of reading Chaucer's verse, then, is to find the five strong stresses and to be sure that in his pronunciation – which we shall be examining in a moment – every letter that appears on the page is to be spoken. So, to return to our Knight, we read (ll. 43–5):

> A Knight ther was, and that a worthy man,
> That fro the tyme that he first bigan
> To ryden out, he loved chivalrye ...

The first entry is easy – 'Knight ... was ... that ... worthy ... man' are all heavy stresses; the second line is easy if we note that 'tyme' is two syllables, so the stressed sounds are 'fro ... tyme ... that ... first ... gan'. In the third line, the words 'ryden' and 'loved' are two syllables each, the first being stressed, and the word 'chivalrye' is four syllables, chiv-al-ree-uh, giving the typical extra soft sound at the end of the line to which we referred earlier. If you have any sort of ear for music of whatever kind, if you sing, whistle, dance, you should soon get the knack of picking up the five beats to a line which is the basis of Chaucer's verse in *The Prologue* and much of his other writing.

If you are interested in pursuing this matter further, and start to look at specialized discussions of Chaucer's verse, you will soon encounter another way of treating it, which may cause some confusion. It is barely relevant to *The Prologue*, which can largely be read as described above, but it is worth a brief account partly because it shows Chaucer's links with his 'English' past, and partly because it leads us naturally to our next problem, that of pronunciation.

In Old English verse – the most famous poem to survive in this language is *Beowulf* – the structure of the line is based on a system quite different from that which we have been describing. Each line is in two halves, each half contains two very heavily emphasized sounds, and the halves are bound together by strong alliteration (that is, the repeating of initial consonants). Old English, in which the consonants were very strong indeed, lent itself well to this style, which was also appropriate to the accounts of battle that so often form the theme. Chaucer may have been familiar with this sort of verse, which was still in popular usage, and seems to have adopted it when it was appropriate. A few lines from the account of the tournament in *The Knight's Tale* will show that the alliteration is more important than the syllables:

> Out *b*rest the *b*lood, with *st*erne *st*remes rede,
> With *m*ighty *m*aces the *b*ones they to-*b*reste.
> He *th*urgh the *th*ikkeste of the *th*rong gan *th*reste ...

The pattern of *four* strong sounds is apparent here, and it serves its purpose well. To appreciate it we have, of course, to be able to read it aloud effectively.

Pronunciation is a more difficult matter than scansion, though we have already suggested one simple principle, that all letters should be sounded if possible. Of course, no one can learn to pronounce a language correctly from a book, even if they have taken the trouble to master the mysteries of the phonetic alphabet. An hour with a guide who knows how to speak in Chaucerian fashion is worth a volume of instruction. That is why you will be offered no voluminous instructions here. If you have the help of someone with this skill, you need read no further. If you have not, there are two possibilities. Should you have access to a good library with a record-lending department, or to an audio-visual centre with a good stock of tapes and discs, you may be able to listen to recordings of Chaucer made by experts. Of special interest is one of the earliest attempts to reconstruct Chaucer's speech, made by three scholars – Coghill, Davis and Burrow – which gives a rendering of the text we are studying, *The Prologue* (ARGO RG 401). A number of other recordings have since been made, such as the Caedmon (TC 1008) recording of parts of *The Pardoner's Tale* and *The Nun's Priest's Tale*; of special interest is *1000 Years of English Pronunciation* (LE 7650/55 Lexington), because it gives not only sections of *The Prologue*, but ranges from Old English to the pronunciation of the eighteenth century, thus enabling the student to see Chaucer in a much fuller perspective.

Much here depends upon what resources you may have at your disposal. If you cannot get at any sort of recording or avail yourself of a teacher who has this skill, you still have the resource of your own voice. It is not too hard to try to read a little yourself, and it can be a lot of fun too. There are three things to bear in mind: the language Chaucer uses is a mixture of French and Germanic words, so you will be making French noises and rather guttural German noises; his spelling, odd though it seems, is an indication of the sounds to be made; and the whole character of the speech was much stronger than standard English today – vowels were fuller, consonants powerfully brought out. Glancing through the opening lines of *The Prologue*, a number of words stand out as being of French origin – 'licour', 'vertu', 'melodye', 'corages' – and you will not go far wrong it you give them a French sound (bearing in mind that every syllable is to be spoken, so that 'engendred' is three sounds, as is 'inspired' and 'melodye' is four sounds, the 'y' and 'e' being sounded separately). A number of other words stand out as being, so to speak, native English – 'holt', 'heeth', 'sonne', 'Ram','y-ronne'. These should be spoken in a very full-throated manner – imagine you are a Yorkshireman (unless you are from Lancashire!), think how he would say words like 'sun' and 'run' and you will be on your way. Finally, remember that in words like 'droghte' every sound is spoken – imagine a Scot making that rasping aspirate at the end of the word 'loch' and that gives you the 'gh' of this and many other words; and, of course, speak the soft 'e' at the end to make an extra syllable. You will soon find you are doing better than the Poet Laureate John Dryden, who believed that many of Chaucer's lines contained only four measures instead of five because he simply did not grasp the notion that a letter means a sound. This, by the way, may help you to feel a little less maddened by modern spelling – most of our 'silent' letters were spoken once.

4. The Text, with Notes

Introduction

Anyone studying *The Prologue* who has gone so far as to obtain a copy of this guide will already have a text of the original. Most editions contain an introduction expressing the editor's view of Chaucer, but the chief emphasis is likely to be on the problems of language. Your edition will probably have notes on the page or at the foot of the page, largely to do with explaining the meaning of words or phrases. There is also likely to be a glossary at the back, containing a list of the more difficult words in alphabetical order, and suggesting modern equivalents. Lastly, there may be notes which deal with references, identify places and so on.

Such editions are very useful, but have dangers. We have already mentioned the deplorable quality of the 'translation' frequently offered – stilted, literary English, unnatural to most students, inappropriate to the lively colloquial writing of the author. An additional difficulty is that it is very easy, when you use a text that has a note on most of the 'hard' words actually on the page, to skim the notes as you read the text, pick up, almost subconsciously, the modern word offered, and think you have understood everything (if you know a little of another language and watch a foreign film with short English subtitles, you will probably find yourself thinking with pleasure how much you understand – but you don't: you skim the general sense from the subtitles, and then it is fairly easy to fill out a little from the sound). It is a good idea to try to buy a completely plain text and, from time to time, test yourself by using that and nothing else.

However, assuming that you have these two-edged weapons at your disposal, we propose, in the edition that follows, to concentrate far less on mere language, far more on interpretation and comment. The text is divided into short, manageable passages, each with an introduction at its head. On the facing page you will find notes on points of interest or difficulty, but *not* a great deal of 'translation', which will be reserved for especially difficult or disputed points.

The text used here is essentially that established by the great Chaucerian scholar, W. W. Skeat. Your own text may differ slightly from it in places, particularly in spelling, which was not, of course, standardized at all in Chaucer's own time. The differences are likely to be small ones. There are

34

few 'readings' in *The Prologue* over which there are serious differences of opinion.

We hope, then, that you will be able to use this edition as a supplement to the laborious but necessary task of rendering Chaucer into modern English, and that it will provoke and stimulate further ideas and speculations about the intentions of this deceptively simple-looking writer.

The opening reminds us at once of several marked differences between Chaucer's world and ours. To us, winter is when we put on the central heating and look out our warmer clothes. In Chaucer's day, winter was a time when people died – the old, the sick, the very young, the poor – and many animals died too. The preservation of food, slaughtered in autumn, was rudimentary, stocks of fuel could not be guaranteed to last and, above all, roads were so bad that all travel came to a halt – in Sussex, where these notes are being written, the heavy clays were completely impassable in winter and, indeed, so sticky all the year round that heavy material like stone for building was always carried by water. So spring really was important then – a new promise of life, fertility, mobility after a dark season of mere survival. We may notice other differences too – the Zodiac, not the calendar, indicates the date. To most of us this is merely a mildly amusing series of signs indicating our 'luck' according to our birth-date. To people in the Middle Ages the Zodiac was a precise and important part of astronomy, or astrology, and so of life. Perhaps the most interesting point is that medieval people obviously did a lot more travelling than we might think. They travelled abroad, as well as in England, despite the slowness of movement. If it took two or three days to get to Canterbury from London, in what spirit did they set out to, for instance, the great Spanish shrine of Santiago?

Here biginneth the Book of the Tales of Caunterbury.

Whan that Aprille with his shoures sote
The droghte of Marche hath perced to the rote,
And bathed every veyne in swich licour,
Of which vertu engendred is the flour;
Whan Zephirus eek with his swete breeth   5
Inspired hath in every holt and heeth
The tendre croppes, and the yonge sonne
Hath in the Ram his halfe cours y-ronne,
And smale fowles maken melodye,
That slepen al the night with open yë,   10

We may begin by noting that the style here is a little more elaborate and formal than in most of *The Prologue*, which is very largely in everyday language. The art of rhetoric, of dressing up plain talk in a variety of fancy ways, was at that time learned by all students, and Chaucer here uses some of its tricks, evoking the spring by a classical reference – Zephirus – and the traditional chirrup of birds. The picture is nevertheless based on reality.

1–2 *Whan that Aprille ... perced to the rote*: March is not a very dry month compared with showery April, but often seems so if it is windy: the topsoil soon loses moisture, and medieval ploughs cut a shallow furrow.

3 *veyne*: this is a disputed word – possibly 'vine', rather in the sense of a growing tendril, but more probably the 'veins' of a tree which convey sap.

4 *vertu*: a good example of the earlier sense which helps so often. In Latin the word means 'strength', and that is almost the meaning here – 'power' or 'force' is better.

5 *Zephirus*: this would have been familiar to every educated reader as a gentle wind from the west, and thus, in this country, likely to bring some rain.

8 *in the Ram*: it is easy to misunderstand this, especially if you are born under Aries. Chaucer was working to a calendar that has since been altered to accommodate mistakes made in earlier systems. Aries was then the prominent sign from 12 March to the same date in April, and this means the sun must be in the *second* half-course – that is, it has passed 12 April. It also helps us to understand the 'yonge sonne' (l. 7) to remember that, to Chaucer, the year began at the end of March (as our 'Financial Year' still does).

10 *That slepen al the night with open yë*: an idiomatic way of saying they 'never sleep a wink'.

(So priketh hem nature in hir corages):
Than longen folk to goon on pilgrimages
(And palmers for to seken straunge strondes)
To ferne halwes, couthe in sondry londes;
And specially, from every shires ende
Of Engelond, to Caunterbury they wende,
The holy blisful martir for to seke,
That hem hath holpen, whan that they were seke.

11 *corages*: French helps here. The root of the word is obviously the French for 'heart', from which, of course, the modern sense of 'courage' is derived.

Our first grammatical point may be made here: where we add an '- s' to the third person singular, 'prick*s*', Chaucer writes 'prik*eth*'.

13 *And palmers for to seken straunge strondes*: as to the sense of 'palmers', pilgrims to the Holy Land wore a bit of palm-leaf in their hats to show that they had been there, rather as some motorists deck their cars with stickers to tell us where they have travelled. A 'stronde' is a 'strand', or 'shore'; the London Strand once ran alongside a rather smelly little river.

14 *ferne halwes, couthe*: 'ferne halwes' is our first example of what is called metathesis (that is, the transposing of letters), very obvious in a word like 'bridde', which is 'bird' in modern English, but less obvious in this expression, which means 'foreign hallowed [that is, sacred] places' ('hallowed' survives for us in the Lord's Prayer: 'Hallowed be thy name . . .'). In the same line, 'couthe' is of interest, as we now have only the negative, 'uncouth', meaning 'ignorant', '*not* knowing' or '*not* known'.

17 *blisful martir*: 'blisful' is a catch – it means 'blessed', not 'happy' in the popular modern sense. These lines remind us that Thomas à Becket was probably the most popular saint in England, and his shrine was famous for its cures. It remained our chief centre of pilgrimage until Henry VIII had it destroyed in 1538.

In this passage we find a typical assembly-point for pilgrims being briefly described – briefly, because most of Chaucer's hearers would be familiar with the area and the customs. The important route eastwards, leading to the great shrine itself and on to the port of Dover, started south of London Bridge – the only bridge then existing – and inns in Southwark were popular gathering-places for parties of pilgrims who wished to make an early start on a busy road, as these did. The inn, whose name refers to the sort of sleeveless jacket still worn by heralds, was probably built round a courtyard, and the big bedrooms were shared – life was less private then – while the stables would hold some horses for hire. The size of the party, which Chaucer seems to have added up rather casually, was partly for protection, partly for economy: travellers were at risk of robbery or worse, and they could probably contrive some 'bulk-buying' of provisions or accommodation *en route*. Thus quite a varied group of people might find themselves glad of one another's company, which admirably suits Chaucer's purpose.

> Bifel that, in that seson on a day,
> In Southwerk at the Tabard as I lay   20
> Redy to wenden on my pilgrimage
> To Caunterbury with ful devout corage,
> At night was come in-to that hostelrye
> Wel nyne and twenty in a companye,
> Of sondry folk, by aventure y-falle   25
> In felawshipe, and pilgrims were they alle,
> That toward Caunterbury wolden ryde;
> The chambres and the stables weren wyde,
> And wel we weren esed atte beste.
> And shortly, whan the sonne was to reste,   30
> So hadde I spoken with hem everichon,
> That I was of hir felawshipe anon,
> And made forward erly for to ryse,
> To take our wey, ther as I yow devyse

21 *wenden*: 'to go' – note the typical '-en' marking an infinitive form. It can also mark a past tense (e.g., 1.27, 'wolden'), so it is necessary to study the context of the word.

22 *Caunterbury*: the fame of the shrine at Canterbury has already been mentioned. It was so popular a journey that it has given a word to the language: a 'Canterbury gallop' meant a controlled hand-gallop, comfortable for the rider and not too hard on the horse – what we now call, in fact, a 'canter'.

25 *aventure y-falle*: 'aventure' is sometimes tricky. The general sense is of something that happens by chance. We have already referred to the prefix 'y-' to show a past participle, so 'y-falle' is literally 'fallen'.

30 *the sonne was to reste*: note that exact times are not given. The movement of the sun largely governed the tempo of life, and that is all the reference needed.

31 *everichon*: this is an example of a common feature – the telescoped word. In full it is 'every each one', a fairly emphatic expression. We should probably say 'every single one of them'.

But natheles, whyl I have tyme and space,   35
Er that I ferther in this tale pace,
Me thinketh it acordaunt to resoun,
To telle yow al the condicioun
Of ech of hem, so as it semed me,
And whiche they weren, and of what degree;   40
And eek in what array that they were inne:
And at a knight than wol I first biginne.

35 *natheles*: similarly, this is a form that we still use – literally 'not the less', hence 'nevertheless'.

38–42 *To telle yow al ... biginne*: this passage is not easy to transpose into modern English, because several difficult concepts are involved. Chaucer would have studied what was then called 'rhetoric', meaning the skilful use of language, and the textbooks laid down a set of rules for describing a character, some of which we should still follow, whereas others may strike us as odd. So one might begin with the name (Chaucer rarely gives us this), the external appearance, the general air or deportment (haughty, humble and so on), the station in life indicated either by wealth or by rank, and the internal nature, what we usually mean by character. The 'condicioun' of the pilgrims is probably a mixture of outward appearance and inner nature. Their 'degree' is what we should call their social status. This was important in medieval times, and in mentioning it there is no element of snobbery – a term they would scarcely have understood in its modern application, though one aspect of it appears in, for example, the wives of the Guildsmen. Feudal society was a clear system of precedence, and thus very useful for a writer who wished to show precisely someone's position in the world. That, of course, is why it is perfectly natural and proper for Chaucer to begin his description with the Knight (who also tells the first story), because he was the man of highest rank amongst them, and he, his son and their servant thus lead the list. A man's servants formed part of his 'array' just as much as his clothes and the sort of horse he rode. Today we still make quick character judgements based on dress, the sort of car, or cars, someone has, even the modern equivalent of servants, such as expensive labour-saving machinery. Thus we learn 'whiche they weren' – what sort of people they are or were.

The Knight has been dealt with on pp. 24–5, so here we need only recall that he has been variously interpreted as a portrait of an actual person, as a 'type' of vanishing chivalry and even – an extreme view – a satire on what chivalry was supposed to be as compared with the free-booting business it often was.

> A KNIGHT ther was, and that a worthy man, Knight.
> That fro the tyme that he first bigan
> To ryden out, he loved chivalrye, 45
> Trouthe and honour, fredom and curteisye.
> Ful worthy was he in his lordes werre,
> And therto hadde he riden (no man ferre)
> As wel in Cristendom as hethenesse,
> And ever honoured for his worthinesse. 50
> At Alisaundre he was, whan it was wonne;
> Ful ofte tyme he hadde the bord bigonne
> Aboven alle naciouns in Pruce.
> In Lettow hadde he reysed and in Ruce,
> No Cristen man so ofte of his degree. 55
> In Gernade at the sege eek hadde he be
> Of Algezir, and riden in Belmarye.
> At Lyeys was he, and at Satalye,
> Whan they were wonne; and in the Grete See
> At many a noble aryve hadde he be. 60
> At mortal batailles hadde he been fiftene,
> And foughten for our feith at Tramissene
> In listes thryes, and ay slayn his foo.
> This ilke worthy knight had been also
> Somtyme with the lord of Palatye, 65
> Ageyn another hethen in Turkye:

45–6   *chivalrye, trouthe and honour, fredom and curteisye*: these terms
are crucial but almost beyond translation. Chivalry itself, based on the
term for a man on a horse ('cheval'), implied fidelity to a code of
behaviour, generosity and – an important point, expanded at 1.70 – the
courtesy which consists in speaking in the same way and behaving with
equal consideration towards everyone: the contrast was 'vileinye',
which means behaviour typical of someone who was 'vile' or low-
born.

51–66   *At Alisaundre ... Turkye*: students often worry more about
getting the modern names of the campaigns right than about where these
places are or what they signify. Chaucer has not helped by somewhat
confusing the order – Belmarye (modern Benmarin) should go with
Tramissene (modern Tlemcen), both North African towns of commercial importance at that time. If we are to take the portrait as sincere,
the most important thing about all these places is that they were
connected with Christian campaigns. One group, starting with
Granada, refers to the attempted expulsion of the Moors (who were,
of course, Moslems) from Spain and North Africa – hence Granada
itself, Algeciras, Benmarin and Tlemcen. The Teutonic Order of
Knights – we still associate 'Pruce' (Prussia) with militarism – cam-
paigned against the Tartars in Lithuania ('Lettow') and Russia, in
which the Knight seems to have joined them. Perhaps to Chaucer's
readers the most interesting series of campaigns would be those in
Turkey, or Anatolia, under the lord of Balat ('Palatye'), against the
Saracens. Most of the places mentioned in this series were wealthy or
strategically important towns, part of the crusading forays whose supposed purpose was to drive the Moslems out of the Holy Land and
assert influence over the whole of the eastern end of the 'Grete See', or
Mediterranean. That he had been chosen to fight on behalf of his
country in a duel of champions whose outcome would be accepted, thus
avoiding a full-scale battle, would obviously mark him as a man of
exceptional skill in arms. There are contemporary records of such
combats. To give a sense of the time-span, Algeciras surrendered in
1344, Lithuania was Christianized by 1385.

The other great point of interest, often lost in the worries of geography, is the very extensive journeys he had made: only one other
pilgrim is recorded as having covered anything like this sort of distance
– the Wife of Bath! If movement was slow in medieval times, it was also
less urgent, perhaps: when no one can go faster than a good horse takes
them no one is in a hurry.

And evermore he hadde a sovereyn prys.
And though that he were worthy, he was wys,
And of his port as meke as is a mayde.
He never yet no vileinye ne sayde   70
In al his lyf, un-to no maner wight.
He was a verray parfit gentil knight.
But for to tellen yow of his array,
His hors were gode, but he was nat gay.
Of fustian he wered a gipoun   75
Al bismotered with his habergeoun;
For he was late y-come from his viage,
And wente for to doon his pilgrimage.

67   *sovereyn prys*: an outstanding reputation.

69   *port*: demeanour or bearing.

72   *He was a verray parfit gentil knight*: the difficulties of this line have been mentioned on pp. 28–9.

74   *hors*: this word is plural, as we can see from the verb 'were'. Chaucer had several different ways of making plurals, inherited from Old English usage, some of which we retain (the '-en' as in 'children'; the change of vowel in 'teeth'; and the way that 'fish' or 'fishes' can be used as alternatives, though 'horses' is now fixed as the plural).

75–6   *Of fustian ... habergeoun*: the coarse cloth tunic ('gipoun') was worn under a mail coat ('habergeoun'). Such armour, which rusted easily and was hard to clean, marks him as old-fashioned. Nor has he bothered to get the stains of the rust out of his simple attire before going on pilgrimage.

78   *And wente for to doon his pilgrimage*: the wording implies that he *always* went to give thanks after a safe return, which accords with his essentially Christian character.

When Chaucer was about the same age as the Squire, he had held the same position and served abroad. Squires had a rather odd collection of duties. They attended on men of rank, up to and including royalty. Often they were expected to wear the livery of their superior. They acted as valets and served at their master's table. They were also expected to provide him and any distinguished guests with entertainment, such as music, story-telling and singing. Thus the Squire we meet here has the appropriate accomplishments. However, he is also clearly meant to be compared with his father, whose courage and campaign experience he is already showing; but where the old man is simple in dress and apparently limited in artistic and social skills, the young man combines these with military virtues and a fine taste in clothes. It seems we have a picture of Chivalry Old Style and New Style in these two. The tone of the writing is lighter, with a touch or two of humour to mark the contrast.

> With him ther was his sone, a yong SQUYER, Squyer.
> A lovyere, and a lusty bacheler,   80
> With lokkes crulle, as they were leyd in presse.
> Of twenty yeer of age he was, I gesse.
> Of his stature he was of evene lengthe,
> And wonderly deliver, and greet of strengthe.
> And he had been somtyme in chivachye,   85
> In Flaundres, in Artoys, and Picardye,
> And born him wel, as of so litel space,
> In hope to stonden in his lady grace.
> Embrouded was he, as it were a mede
> Al ful of fresshe floures, whyte and rede.   90
> Singinge he was, or floytinge, al the day;
> He was as fresh as is the month of May.
> Short was his goune, with sleves longe and wyde.
> Wel coude he sitte on hors, and faire ryde.

80   *bacheler*: a bachelor did not then mean an unmarried man, any more than it does in the modern university degree. A Bachelor of Arts has the lowest degree and may hope to go higher – the Squire hopes to become a knight. Obviously he is not in fact married, as he is very much a ladies' man.

81   *crulle*: another metathesis – transpose the letters to find the modern word 'curl'.

83   *evene lengthe*: 'of average height'.

84   *And wonderly deliver, and greet of strengthe*: he was both agile *and* strong – not muscle-bound.

86   *In Flaundres, in Artoys, and Picardye*: a reminder that Flanders, linked in our minds with World War I, has been fought over many times. There was campaigning going on in the areas mentioned about 1385, a part of that long background struggle between England and France known as the Hundred Years War, referred to on p. 11.

88   *In hope to stonden in his lady grace*: he fought well to gain favour with a lady, natural in a young man. A point of grammatical interest is that in Old English some nouns did not make their possessive form by adding ''s', and this is one which survives, as we still call 25 March 'Lady Day', not 'Lady's Day'.

89–93   *Embrouded ... wyde*: the dress is interesting not merely because it is showy but because it carries a conventional symbolism. The references to a meadow and the colours white and red indicated spring-time, born out by the comparison with May, and the word 'fresh' was very often applied to young people, so that we might translate it as 'youthful', or 'lively'. The Squire is in the springtime of life. The short gown was to show off his thighs (as we still do in full evening dress with our cutaway tail-coat) and the long sleeves showed that he did not work. Impracticality is often a feature of high fashion.

94   *Sitte ... ryde*: the two verbs are distinct – he had a good seat on a horse and he could manage it well. A good rider does not always sit elegantly.

He coude songes make and wel endyte,   95
Juste and eek daunce, and wel purtreye and wryte.
So hote he lovede, that by nightertale
He sleep namore than dooth a nightingale.
Curteys he was, lowly, and servisable,
And carf biforn his fader at the table.   100

95–6 *He coude ... wryte*: as we have noted, these accomplishments would be useful in the discharge of his duties as well as attractive in themselves. To his singing and flute-playing is thus added the ability to devise the words and compose the music of songs; jousting was hard and dangerous, dancing was often quite athletic; sketching portraits would doubtless be an entertainment for the subjects, and, we are told, he could write down his compositions himself. Literacy, outside the Church (see the Clerk), was not common. Even great nobles often had others to read and write for them, and sealed their documents or scrawled their names, perhaps the only writing they knew. The Squire writes well. Medieval handwriting was laborious.

97–8 *So hote ... nightingale*: deliberately ambiguous. We do not know if he was kept awake by frustration, consummation or singing serenades. Sleeplessness was a recognized symptom of love, and some people would still so regard it.

100 *And carf biforn his fader at the table*: as we have seen, to serve at table was an expected duty. Carving the great joints of the time was a real skill.

The Yeoman completes the little aristocratic party very neatly in every way. He is a neat man himself, in build and habits, and he complements his master. Normally a knight might be expected to be attended by a cavalcade of armed retainers and other servants. Our Knight is a modest man who abhors show, and a pious one who would think it inappropriate to go on pilgrimage in any but the humblest style. Since his son will attend to his personal needs as part of his ordinary duties, he takes with him a single, workmanlike fellow. The character is not presented as an individual, but as a reflection of the man he serves.

A yeoman today means a farmer of modest position as compared with someone who owns an estate. In Chaucer's day this sense was well established, with a more general one of someone quietly prosperous and independent. Some details here suggest that the Yeoman was not without means of his own but had accompanied the Knight on campaign, though his close-cropped hair was the mark of a servant. He might have been a tenant of a farm on the Knight's estate, where he also served as a forester, an important position in those times of strict preservation of game, when hunting was the chief outdoor activity of the aristocrat.

> A YEMAN hadde he, and servaunts namo   Yeman.
> At that tyme, for him liste ryde so;
> And he was clad in cote and hood of grene;
> A sheef of pecok-arwes brighte and kene
> Under his belt he bar ful thriftily;   105
> (Wel coude he dresse his takel yemanly:
> His arwes drouped noght with fetheres lowe),
> And in his hand he bar a mighty bowe.
> A not-heed hadde he, with a broun visage.
> Of wode-craft wel coude he al the usage.   110

101   *A Yeman hadde he, and servaunts namo*: as we have no real equivalent in modern English, it is usual merely to modernize the spelling of
'Yeman' and refer to the 'Yeoman'. 'Namo' is another contraction: 'no
more'.

102   *him liste*: this represents a very common construction in Chaucer,
the impersonal. We should say 'he chose' or 'he wished', but Chaucer
said '(it) was wished to him'. Many verbs were so used, and a good
example of one that has survived is 'it seems to me' rather than the
personal 'I think'.

103   *grene*: he wears green probably because of his work as a forester –
a sort of gamekeeper-cum-huntsman.

104   *pecok-arwes*: the sense of the peacock-feather reference is disputed.
Authorities have been cited to suggest that the peacock feather was
rather unsuitable and made the arrow liable to drop in flight, but the
Yeoman set his arrow-feathers so well that he avoided this; alterna-
tively, that they were the best feathers, and others were considered 'low'
by comparison.

108   *bowe*: the bow is obviously a longbow, the weapon that had proved
so devastating in earlier battles in France – Crécy in particular.

110   *coude*: this is an example of a word having a fuller meaning in
Chaucer's time than it has now.

Upon his arm he bar a gay bracer,
And by his syde a swerd and a bokeler,
And on that other syde a gay daggere,
Harneised wel, and sharp as point of spere;
A Cristofre on his brest of silver shene.   115
An horn he bar, the bawdrik was of grene;
A forster was he, soothly, as I gesse.

111–15 *Upon his arm ... silver shene*: the terms and equipment of archery have changed little. A bracer is a guard worn on the left arm to protect it against the string. Of his equipment we notice that much of it is not plain – the bracer is 'gay', as is the dagger, and the latter is 'harneised wel', implying that its sheath and hangings were decorated. The image of St Christopher is also of 'shining silver'. Generally, the picture is of someone who is very businesslike, very professional, as we might say, about his job, but who can afford to have his excellent equipment handsomely ornamented. Thus the idea of the Yeoman as a man of some substance, not a mere servant, is reinforced.

St Christopher, the patron saint of foresters, is still popular as a protector of travellers, though the Church of Rome has recently disowned him, along with some other popular figures like St Valentine. The implication here is surely that the Yeoman has been on or was accustomed to going on long journeys. Probably we are to assume that he had been overseas with his master, where his skill with the bow would have stood him in good stead, and that is why he is the one man chosen to escort him on this journey of thanksgiving for a safe return.

116 *bawdrik*: this survives as 'baldric' in modern English, a belt slung across one shoulder, but is rather a literary word; 'sling' would satisfy most readers.

117 *as I gesse*: Chaucer was not above padding out a line occasionally just to get a rhyme or rhythm. Thus the 'guess' has no special significance. Everything about the Yeoman suggests the likelihood of his being employed in this way – the brown visage, green, simple clothes, well-kept archery equipment – and we are being invited to share the assumption that that is what he was.

The Prioress is one of the most admired pictures in the gallery, and may be one of the most misunderstood. A crucial question, impossible to determine, is her social standing. She may well have been of a minor aristocratic family, and we have to remember that such women were a very real liability to their parents. If a good match could not be found – and this meant a handsome dowry had to go with the bride – there was really nothing for them to do. They could not work for a living, so they either lingered on as vaguely helpful spinsters in the households of their relatives, or entered the Church as nuns. Some of the convents were quite small and not particularly pious, but probably quite pleasant places for such women to live in in an atmosphere of chatter and rather lax observation of the official rules.

The character-drawing of this lady is celebrated as a striking example of Chaucer's indirect method – the word 'sly' is favoured by many editors, but carries the wrong implications.

Ther was also a Nonne, a PRIORESSE,	Prioresse.
That of hir smyling was ful simple and coy;	
Hir gretteste ooth was but by sëynt Loy;	120
And she was cleped madame Eglentyne.	
Ful wel she song the service divyne,	
Entuned in hir nose ful semely;	
And Frensh she spak ful faire and fetisly,	
After the scole of Stratford atte Bowe,	125
For Frensh of Paris was to hir unknowe.	
At mete wel y-taught was she with-alle;	
She leet no morsel from hir lippes falle,	
Ne wette hir fingres in hir sauce depe.	
Wel coude she carie a morsel, and wel kepe,	130
That no drope ne fille up-on hir brest.	
In curteisye was set ful muche hir lest.	
Hir over lippe wyped she so clene,	
That in hir coppe was no ferthing sene	
Of grece, whan she dronken hadde hir draughte.	135
Ful semely after hir mete she raughte,	

119 *coy*: the word now carries a sense of pretended modesty, but here it means 'demure'.

120 *Hir gretteste ooth was but by sëynt Loy*: much ink has been spilt on St Eligius or Eloi or Loy. He was popular in Flanders, where Edward III's Queen Philippa came from. Of course the Prioress should not have sworn at all: perhaps there is the implication that she swore a mild lady-like oath, which fits her other manners; or it may be a way of saying that she did not swear.

121 *Eglentyne*: this is wrong for a nun, who renounces her worldly name when she takes the veil and adopts a religious one instead. It is rather a fancy name, too, used for the sweet-briar or the honeysuckle. But 'madame' was correct.

123 *Entuned in hir nose ful semely*: was her singing affected, or does this nasal tone refer to a way of chanting the long services without tiring the throat? Nobody knows, but we should not be too ready to suggest affectation.

124–6 *And Frensh ... unknowe*: her French is also a matter for debate. The Stratford referred to suggests that she had attended a Benedictine convent at Bromley, West Ham. Perhaps the French there had something of a local twang as distinct from court French, which was more like that of Paris, or the Norman-French which was now old-fashioned. The general suggestion is that she was rather pretentious, and her accent may have betrayed her pretensions, or defined the class to which she wished to be thought to belong.

127 *mete*: this word meant any foodstuff, as in 'sweetmeat'. There follows a vivid account, by implication, of what ordinary table manners must have been like. Forks were not in common use, so when the fragment of meat or other food was dipped into the central bowl of sauce, there was a skill in doing it quickly and neatly, like dunking a doughnut.

129 *depe*: note that 'depe' means 'deeply' – the food had to be lightly dipped.

132 *curteisye*: here the word means 'etiquette', or the outward forms of polite behaviour.

133–5 *Hir over lippe ... draughte*: the cup was passed round, and to receive it after a gross feeder in an age when fat meat was esteemed (for its heat-giving properties) must have been a greasily unpleasant experience. There is surely no satire in saying that she took care not to offend others in this way. Older students may recall the size of a farthing, and see why this tiny coin is used to describe a small round spot. It was a 'fourthing' of the old penny.

57

And sikerly she was of greet disport,
And ful plesaunt, and amiable of port,
And peyned hir to countrefete chere
Of court, and been estatlich of manere,   140
And to ben holden digne of reverence.
But, for to speken of hir conscience,
She was so charitable and so pitous,
She wolde wepe, if that she sawe a mous
Caught in a trappe, if it were deed or bledde.   145
Of smale houndes had she, that she fedde
With rosted flesh, or milk and wastel-breed.
But sore weep she if oon of hem were deed,
Or if men smoot it with a yerde smerte:
And al was conscience and tendre herte.   150

137–40   *And sikerly ... Of court*: that she was entertaining company may have made her a pleasant fellow-traveller, but nuns were not supposed to engage in unnecessary talk of any kind, or to be sociable in behaviour ('amiable of port'). The vow of obedience meant total subjugation of your own personality to the Order, so her efforts to imitate ('countre-fete' suggests they were not genuine) the manners of the court and to put on a superior style of behaviour to try to gain social esteem were in breach of her vow, and would, in any case, be mildly amusing in themselves, if harmless enough. However, at this point the lightly satirical manner takes on a more serious tone.

142–50   *But ... tendre herte*: her 'conscience' is now examined. The vow of poverty meant that a nun had no personal possessions at all – even her habit belonged to the Order, so she certainly should not have had lap-dogs. All her feelings are for animals – the mouse in the trap, the spoilt dog given a smart wallop – and her charity is for her pets: there is something almost obscene about their diet. Many of the labouring folk of England virtually never ate meat at all, milk had to be made into cheese as a staple diet and 'wastel-breed' made of the finest flour was a luxury for the rich, the poor subsisting on the so-called 'black' bread made of rye or barley or even beans, peas and anything else edible that could be roughly ground up. All her 'tenderness of heart' is for beasts, not people. The type is not unfamiliar today.

Ful semely hir wimpel pinched was;
Hir nose tretys; hir eyen greye as glas;
Hir mouth ful smal, and ther-to softe and reed;
But sikerly she hadde a fair forheed;
It was almost a spanne brood, I trowe;   155
For, hardily, she was nat undergrowe.
Ful fetis was hir cloke, as I was war.
Of smal coral aboute hir arm she bar
A peire of bedes, gauded al with grene;
And ther-on heng a broche of gold ful shene,   160
On which ther was first write a crowned A,
And after, *Amor vincit omnia.*

Another NONNE with hir hadde she,   Nonne.
That was hir chapeleyne, and PREESTES three.   3 Preestes.

151–62 *Ful semely* ... omnia: the account of her appearance is also satirical, though she seems to have been good-looking enough. Grey eyes, with a shine in them like glass, were fashionable, a well-shaped nose and delicate mouth are pleasing attributes, but we do not, like medieval men, relish a high forehead. If you have seen old paintings, it may have struck you that the women's heads look like eggs. If the forehead was not high enough, it was often shaved back a little. But the point is that this excellent feature should be covered – if you look at a modern nun you may see she wears a coif, a white band low on the brow. The Prioress must have pushed hers up – and also played a few tricks to make her wimple, part of the same headgear, look pretty. Chaucer praises her for features that she should not be displaying at all.

A nun today is likely to have a rosary at her belt, and you will usually see that it is black, and certainly that it is plain. The Prioress is commended for her handsome 'paire of bedes' of colourful coral: this is clearly a rosary – 'to pray' or 'to bid' was so often associated with a string of counting devices that they themselves became called 'beads', though the word meant 'prayers'. A rosary is arranged in groups of ten (for each of which you say a 'Hail Mary') followed by a bigger bead, then called a 'gaude', for which you say an 'Our Father' before going on to the next ten 'Hail Marys'. Here the big beads are green, to add more colour to this religious trinket, which should end in a crucifix, not an expensive bright gold clasp with a fancy motto and design. The Latin – 'Love conquers all' – originally appears in a poem by Virgil, and referred to human love, but it was accepted as equally applicable to the love of God. As the Prioress is so vain, so spinsterish with her lap-dogs and fussy with her manners, it seems absurd to suggest that she wore the brooch as a sort of signal to would-be admirers (but compare the Monk in this respect). She simply should not have had such fancy personal adornments.

163–4 *Another Nonne* ... *Preestes three*: while a woman could be a 'chapeleyne' and look after conventual administration, only a priest could say Mass. For High Mass three were needed: priest, deacon and subdeacon.

The first monastery had been founded by St Benedict ('Beneit' in Chaucer) over nine hundred years before *The Prologue* was written, and the Benedictines are familiar to us still, if only, for many of us, in their famous liqueur. One of his earliest (and shadowiest) adherents was St Maurus ('Maure'), and St Augustine ('Austin'), who lived earlier, had extolled in a letter to a local convent the virtue of hard, physical labour, which was adopted by the more austere monasteries. The code of practice ('reule') which Benedict laid down, and which became the basis for monastic life generally as other Orders were founded, was to keep strictly to a fixed routine of prayer, praise and work, to live an austere life and, in the case of the enclosed Orders, not to leave the monastery at all once you had taken your vows. For those to whom monastic life is a mystery, it should be explained that in Roman Catholic teaching we can all help to alleviate the suffering of souls in Purgatory by prayer; so a primary function of monks and nuns was regular worship on behalf of other people – a life wholly devoted to God for the sake of one's fellows. Monasteries also became centres of learning, often acted as local dispensaries to sick people, gave shelter to poor travellers and were, ideally, self-supporting by the labour of all the members. Over a millennium, good intentions may become corrupt, and a lot of monasteries had become prosperous and idle, though probably we have a distorted view of how corrupt they were, since critics were always ready to attack the bad ones and keep silent about those, probably a majority, that still kept up a decent level of religious observance. However, there was a growing feeling that the cloistered life was all too comfortably remote from reality. The Monk himself certainly does not care for it, and is really leading a thoroughly worldly life.

A MONK ther was, a fair for the maistrye,	Monk.
An out-rydere, that lovede venerye;	166
A manly man, to been an abbot able.	
Ful many a deyntee hors hadde he in stable:	
And, whan he rood, men mighte his brydel here	
Ginglen in a whistling wind as clere,	170
And eek as loude as dooth the chapel-belle,	
Ther as this lord was keper of the celle.	
The reule of seint Maure or of seint Beneit,	
By-cause that it was old and som-del streit,	
This ilke monk leet olde thinges pace,	175
And held after the newe world the space.	

165 *fair for the maistrye*: this is a literal translation of French idiom –
'the very best'.

166 *An out-rydere, that lovede venerye*: the monasteries had to have
some members who could leave the premises – for example to oversee
their often large estates. This is the Monk's job. His love of 'venerye'
appears to refer to hunting, but it is ambiguous, perhaps even a pun,
since the word could also mean (compare it with Venus and venereal)
what we sum up as 'sex'. In the next line we are told he was a 'manly'
man, and this emphasizes his virility. He should, of course, have been
celibate in thought and act.

168–72 *Ful many ... celle*: his highly bred horses and heavily ornamented harness that jingles as he rides are both signs of wealth and
personal possessions. There may be another pun in 'keper of the celle',
which could mean that he was in charge of a small religious community
or, ironically, that he spent most of his time in his cell, as Scots still
speak of 'keeping the house' meaning to stay in: in fact he seems to have
spent precious little time there. The bell too may remind us of all the
services that he missed.

174 *streit*: this means 'strict' or 'narrow', the latter sense surviving as
in Straits of Dover. The passage which follows is heavily ironic –
Chaucer echoes the Monk's words with apparent approval when clearly
he felt the man was a sham. He is in effect reproducing the Monk's own
glib excuses: 'Let old-fashioned ways go, I'm all for keeping up with
the times.' See also the note to l. 183.

He yaf nat of that text a pulled hen,
That seith, that hunters been nat holy men;
Ne that a monk, whan he is cloisterlees,
Is lykned til a fish that is waterlees;   180
This is to seyn, a monk out of his cloistre.
But thilke text held he nat worth an oistre;
And I seyde, his opinioun was good.
What sholde he studie, and make him-selven wood,
Upon a book in cloistre alwey to poure,   185
Or swinken with his handes, and laboure,
As Austin bit? How shal the world be served?
Lat Austin have his swink to him reserved.
Therfore he was a pricasour aright;
Grehoundes he hadde, as swifte as fowel in flight;   190

177–81 *He yaf nat ... cloistre*: the word 'text' here is a pitfall. When we use the word, we generally mean a quotation from the Bible, often used as the basis of a sermon. Psalm 90 refers to Esau, who was a hunter, as a sinner, and Nimrod, the 'mighty hunter' of the Old Testament, was held up as an example of a destroyer of creatures brought into being by God. The comparison of the fish out of water and the monk out of his cloister was a familiar one (in Latin) and was quoted or used by a number of medieval writers in attacks on monasteries. The word could thus mean a well-known saying or a commentary made by one of the early theologians, such as St Jerome, who used Esau to illustrate what he thought to be God's attitude to hunters. Hunting was associated with the aristocracy, who jealously preserved their rights. Something of this survives today in the Game Laws, though a hundred years ago these were far more severe. The picture is slowly being built up of a man who, under the comfortable cloak of a position with a religious house that gave him the right to move freely, was living an utterly worldly life, was rich and self-indulgent, and whose chief activity was one proper to the nobility. What is worse, he openly scoffs at the strict, old-fashioned rules he is supposed to maintain. This treatment is much harsher than that given to the Prioress.

182 *oistre*: not then a luxury. If you lived near a suitable river, they were common fare.

183 *seyde*: this is past tense, so Chaucer is telling us he *agreed* with him at the time they were talking together, not that he *agrees* with the view.

184 *wood*: a well-known catch. There were two words, quite unconnected, one meaning 'wood' as used today, the other, as here, 'crazy'.

186 *swinken*: this has the infinitive '-en' and is a word that has vanished without trace. It meant 'to work hard with your hands', 'to labour'.

187 *Austin*: see the Introduction to the Monk on p. 62.

Of priking and of hunting for the hare
Was al his lust, for no cost wolde he spare.
I seigh his sleves purfiled at the hond
With grys, and that the fyneste of a lond;
And, for to festne his hood under his chin,   195
He hadde of gold y-wroght a curious pin:
A love-knotte in the gretter ende ther was.
His heed was balled, that shoon as any glas,
And eek his face, as he had been anoint.
He was a lord ful fat and in good point;   200
His eyen stepe, and rollinge in his heed,
That stemed as a forneys of a leed;
His botes souple, his hors in greet estat.
Now certeinly he was a fair prelat;
He was nat pale as a for-pyned goost.   205
A fat swan loved he best of any roost.
His palfrey was as broun as is a berye.

191   *priking*: the word means 'tracking' – in the technical language of the hunt, the mark which the hare left with its paw was called a 'prick'. Some commentators have suspected a bawdy pun here, in view of the other suggestions that the Monk is interested in other game, or another game, but this seems far-fetched: the hare was much hunted because it ran fast, it ran in a circle, so it would require a clever rider to be in at the kill, and it made a nice rich dish. It still does.

193–204   *I seigh his sleves . . . fair prelat*: his dress, it is obvious, was far removed from the austere habit of the Benedictines. His sleeves are edged with fur, a comfort that was forbidden in the rules, and 'grys' – literally 'grey fur' – was costly. He should not have had a brooch, let alone a 'curious' – that is, 'elaborate' – one made of gold, for personal adornment was not allowed. While we may be unsure of the meaning of the inscription on the Prioress's brooch and give her the benefit of the doubt, a 'love-knotte', a complex knot signifying that two people are inextricably intertwined, could not possibly have a religious meaning. The Monk likes women. In the medieval mind good food and being highly sexed went together, so it is no surprise to learn at this point that he shone as if anointed with oil – he is so well-fed he sweats it out – that his eyes bulged, that his perspiring bald pate steamed like a fire under a cauldron ('leed') and that he was 'in good point', which sounds more like a description of a prime ox, 'in first-class condition'. His horses are as well fed as he, 'in greet estat'. He rode in expensive boots of supple leather, and certainly he was a fine-*looking* cleric, but, as we have seen, everything about him is wrong.

205   *for-pyned goost*: the prefix 'for' intensifies the meaning – 'wasted away by torments' would probably convey the full sense, since a 'goost' was a spirit, and the image seems to be of a damned soul in hell. There may be just a hint here that one day that is exactly what this self-indulgent hypocrite will be. In an age when many starved, gluttony (overeating) was a mortal sin – that is, one that condemned you to hell if you did not repent and secure forgiveness.

206–7   *A fat swan . . . berye*: the last touches seem more random than they are. Swans were costly, large and greasy to eat (hence, perhaps, his 'anointed' face), and a palfrey was a quiet horse, suitable for ladies and clergy. He would not ride one of his fancy hunters when merely hacking down to Canterbury.

Of the three 'Church' characters introduced here, Chaucer clearly had most sympathy for the Prioress, least for the Friar. We have to be clear about the difference between a Monk – essentially one who lived in a monastery a life of regular prayer – and a Friar – one who went out into the world, as poorly clad as Christ's own disciples, and preached. The four Orders referred to are the Black Friars, or Dominicans, the Franciscans, or Grey Friars, the White Friars, or Carmelites, and the Augustinians, or Austin Friars. The first three often turn up in names of streets in old cities. St Francis is well known to most of us, and his example of poverty, humility and simplicity was supposed to be the ideal. Poverty meant that they could beg – indeed, often had to. As they sometimes needed accommodation, they built friaries, which soon became large and wealthy. Friars were popular because they preached, and medieval folk enjoyed the spoken word, and because they would carry out many of the duties of a priest as well. On the other hand, they were unpopular, and the subject of many of the accusations which Chaucer makes, because they had easy access to all sorts of households, in particular to women, and got a lot of free food and drink. To be a successful friar – as distinct from a sincerely religious one – you had to be good at pleasing all sorts of people. Our Friar is a smooth-tongued rogue. To balance the picture, we ought to know that many members of the four Orders were men of learning and played their part in the development of the universities at a time when the monastic contribution to scholarship was declining. Chaucer's picture is not exactly prejudiced – he simply repeats the popular view.

> A FRERE ther was, a wantown and a merye,   Frere.
> A limitour, a ful solempne man.
> In alle the ordres, foure is noon that can   210
> So muche of daliaunce and fair langage.
> He hadde maad ful many a mariage
> Of yonge wommen, at his owne cost.
> Un-to his ordre he was a noble post.
> Ful wel biloved and famulier was he   215
> With frankeleyns over-al in his contree,
> And eek with worthy wommen of the toun:
> For he had power of confessioun,
> As seyde him-self, more than a curat,
> For of his ordre he was licentiat.   220

208   *wantown*: this is a word of wide suggestion. At its most harmless, it means he was sociable; at its worst, it means he was sexually promiscuous. The implication is that he was both.

209   *limitour*: a friar who had a licence to beg within a limited area.

210   *ordres foure*: for the Orders, see the introduction to this passage on p. 68.

212–13   *He hadde maad ... owne cost*: this is ambiguous. Generously, he may have married without fee, but the rest of the portrait suggests he married off girls who had accommodated him, since they could not be married to him – a parting gift on pregnancy?

216   *frankeleyns*: we shall, of course, meet a franklin later. These were men who were not aristocrats, but held property freehold. They were thus very independent and lived well. Obviously they were useful friends to have.

218–20   *For he had ... licentiat*: friars could be licensed to hear confessions, and he is 'licenciat'. He *claims*, however, that he is better qualified than a curate or parish priest. This means he could give absolution for much more serious sins.

Ful swetely herde he confessioun,
And plesaunt was his absolucioun;
He was an esy man to yeve penaunce
Ther as he wiste to han a good pitaunce;
For unto a povre ordre for to yive   225
Is signe that a man is well y-shrive.
For if he yaf, he dorste make avaunt,
He wiste that a man was repentaunt.
For many a man so hard is of his herte,
He may nat wepe al-thogh him sore smerte.   230
Therfore, in stede of weping and preyeres,
Men moot yeve silver to the povre freres.
His tipet was ay farsed ful of knyves
And pinnes, for to yeven faire wyves.
And certeinly he hadde a mery note;   235
Wel coude he singe and pleyen on a rote.

223   *esy man to yeve penaunce*: this explains why he made the claim and
why 'worthy' women liked him to hear their confessions. He did not
give hard penances – that is, punishments which the penitent had to
accept as part of the process of being absolved, or forgiven. 'Yeve'
means 'give'. The letter 'y' sometimes represents its modern sound,
sometimes a 'g' as here. It comes from an Old English letter, written
rather like a script 'z', which had two different pronunciations and
sometimes led to the formation of two different words in later times.
Thus most of us know Constable's picture 'The Hay Wain', but do we
recognize that 'wain' is the other form of 'wagon'? With an unfamiliar
word containing a 'y' it is useful to try both ways of sounding it.

224   *Ther as he wiste*: where he thought he would get a handsome
contribution; here, probably a good meal. He absolved people with a
mere token penance (saying a few prayers, for example) if they would
pay him in cash or kind. Officially money went to the Order, and at
lines 225–6 we catch an echo of his sales-talk: 'To give generously to
a poor order is a clear indication that a man has been properly penitent
and absolved.'

227–32   *For if he yaf ... povre freres*: more reported sales-patter. The
Friar persuasively tells his customers that there are some people who
are so hardened that they cannot express their grief at their wrong-
doing by tears, however much their guilt hurts them (note another
impersonal form in the construction 'him sore smerte'). So, says the
plausible Friar, if you can't show how sorry you are by tears and
prayers, you can always do it by a contribution to the poor friars. To give
to them is an act of charity that will be recorded to your credit in heaven.

The whole of this passage is, of course, an attack on the abuse of
confession. People were virtually being invited to buy off God and sin
again, so long as they could pay. It is essential to true confession that
we resolve to try never to repeat the offence, and that we are genuinely
sorry we have committed it. To the Friar it's a cash transaction. Worse,
he encourages others to see it so, as does the Summoner.

233-4   *His tipet ... faire wyves*: a 'tipet' was a part of the universally
worn hood, with folds or pockets. 'Farsed' is 'stuffed', as in modern
'forcemeat'. The knives and pins would be fancy ones, the pins more
like brooches perhaps. We still speak of 'pin money' to describe a
woman's allowance for small items of personal adornment. Note that
only 'faire' – that is, 'pretty' – women got these presents.

236   *rote*: there are different opinions as to which musical instrument this
was, but it was certainly stringed, possibly a small kind of fiddle easily
carried.

71

Of yeddinges he bar utterly the prys.
His nekke whyt was as the flour-de-lys;
Ther-to he strong was as a champioun.
He knew the tavernes wel in every toun,   240
And everich hostiler and tappestere
Bet than a lazar or a beggestere;
For un-to swich a worthy man as he
Acorded nat, as by his facultee,
To have with seke lazars aqueyntaunce.   245
It is nat honest, it may nat avaunce
For to delen with no swich poraille,
But al with riche and sellers of vitaille.
And over-al, ther as profit sholde aryse,
Curteys he was, and lowly of servyse.   250
Ther nas no man no-wher so vertuous.
He was the beste beggere in his hous;
[And yaf a certeyn ferme for the graunt;   ⌐252*b*
Noon of his bretheren cam ther in his haunt;]   252*c*⌐
For thogh a widwe hadde noght a sho,
So plesaunt was his '*In principio*,'
Yet wolde he have a ferthing, er he wente.   255
His purchas was wel bettre than his rente.
And rage he coude, as it were right a whelpe.
In love-dayes ther coude he muchel helpe.
For there he was nat lyk a cloisterer,
With a thredbar cope, as is a povre scoler,   260
But he was lyk a maister or a pope.
Of double worsted was his semi-cope,
That rounded as a belle out of the presse.
Somwhat he lipsed, for his wantownesse,
To make his English swete up-on his tonge;   265
And in his harping, whan that he had songe,
His eyen twinkled in his heed aright,
As doon the sterres in the frosty night.
This worthy limitour was cleped Huberd.

237 *yeddinges*: this word has been variously translated as 'ballads', 'proverbs' and 'improvised verses'. We might settle for 'improvised songs', since his musical and social gifts are much stressed. Such songs were generally narrative.

241 *tappestere*: note the 'e', which here shows a feminine – 'barmaid' or 'woman publican'.

244–8 *Acorded nat ... sellers of vitaille*: here again Chaucer invites us, so to speak, to listen to the way the Friar argued his case. It is not honourable – or profitable! – to mix with such rubbish as lepers and beggars. This is the opposite of the teaching of Christ, which he was supposed to follow. Christ worked amongst the poor and helped the sick, but the Friar mixes only with rich people, always looking for cash.

250 *Curteys he was, and lowly of servyse*: is this line a deliberate echo of the description of the Squire at 1. 99? He has some of the Squire's gifts, but they are put to base uses: to make profit and to attract married women, it seems.

252*b*–252*c* *And yaf ... his haunt*: your text may not contain these lines, which are probably not part of the original. They say, in effect, that he had paid a lump sum for the right to work his territory, and was making a profit on it.

254 'In principio': this is Latin for 'In the beginning', the opening of St John's Gospel and used by friars as a greeting on entering a house. The widow so poor that she had no shoes from whom he nevertheless squeezed a farthing may remind us of the story of the Widow's Mite, the farthing being all she had. He is not only a skilled beggar, but a heartless one.

256 *rente*: this is a tricky word, and meant 'income' at this period. He made more in perks than the income permitted him by his Order.

258 *love-dayes*: these were originally days for settling disputes amicably without recourse to the courts. This excellent idea had lent itself to much abuse. The Friar, dressed up like a Master of Divinity or the Pope himself instead of in the plain habit of his Order, is in his element – and making a lot of money – on these occasions.

264 *lipsed*: this is a metathesis for 'lisped', implying, with 'wantownesse', an affected style of speech. Con-men have to be persuasive.

269 *This worthy limitour was cleped Huberd*: Chaucer rounds off this harsh portrait of a man who wholly betrays the faith which he professes to serve by saying what a worthy example of it he was, and, for the first time in *The Prologue*, gives us a character's name. As it was an uncommon one, there may be a reference here that we have lost.

Leaving the aristocracy and the Church, Chaucer here turns to the first of what we might call the middle-class figures. It is not easy to assess his attitude to men like this. The merchants were a rising class, and this he might have resented; all businessmen have to be a little sharp in their practice from time to time if they are to succeed, and of this he might have disapproved: yet his own father was, in a sense, in 'trade', as the Victorians disdainfully called it, and it is hard to see, as some have done, a ferocious attack on greed and dishonesty in this portrait. True, the man is showy, rather a bore and interested only in money. His Flemish hat might be fashionable, but Chaucer had lived through a time when immigrant Flemish workers had been hounded down the streets of London and killed for taking jobs away from Englishmen. There have even been attempts – based on the curious assumption that he claimed not to know his name because his hearers would not need to be told it – to identify him as someone Chaucer met in his work in Customs. You may think, on the other hand, that this is just a typical portrait of a successful businessman, probably trading chiefly in wool, with various mildly shady dealings on the side. He tells what most people would agree to be one of the most unpleasant of all the tales, but travelling businessmen are still reputed to have a stock of such things as part of their good-fellowship act.

> A MARCHANT was ther with a forked berd,   Marchant.
> In mottelee, and hye on horse he sat,   271
> Up-on his heed a Flaundrish bever hat;
> His botes clasped faire and fetisly.
> His resons he spak ful solempnely,
> Souninge alway thencrees of his winning.   275
> He wolde the see were kept for any thing
> Bitwixe Middelburgh and Orewelle.
> Wel coude he in eschaunge sheeldes selle.
> This worthy man ful wel his wit bisette;
> Ther wiste no wight that he was in dette,   280

271   *In mottelee, and hye on horse he sat*: to us 'motley' suggests the red and yellow of the jester, but it means simply a mixture of colours – he is a rather showy dresser. That he sat 'hye' on his horse may mean he rode with a sort of arrogant swagger, or that he had a lively horse which pranced a good deal.

273   *His botes clasp ed faire and fetisly*: we may notice how often footwear is mentioned. Good riding-boots which fit well – the implication of saying they were clasped attractively and neatly – were, and are, expensive.

274–5   *His resons ... winning*: 'souninge alway thencrees' is slightly ambiguous. It could mean that whatever the conversation it always tended to turn towards the profits he made, or that he talked about public affairs ('resons' would be his opinions on such matters) as they affected his own business successes. The two versions overlap in sense in any case.

276   *kept*: this means 'guarded' as in modern 'keeper', a guardian or the like.

277   *Middelburgh and Orewelle*: we can modernize Orwell, still the name of a river, to Harwich, which is near to where the old port stood. Middleburg, as we should now spell it, is on the Dutch island of Walcheren. The passage is of interest to scholars because the Wool Staple, the place authorized by statute to trade in wool, one of the staple products of the period, was at Middleburg from 1384 to 1388, and it thus seems that the merchant dealt in wool. Furthermore, it gives us a convenient reference for dating the composition of the passage. Piracy has existed for as long as men have carried goods by sea, and the Channel was subject to raids from various quarters, including Scotland.

278   *sheeldes*: French coins, literally *écus*. The Merchant was able to make a profit on currency exchanges – illegally, however, since only the Royal Exchange had this right.

280   *Ther wiste no wight that he was in dette*: he was clever enough to ensure that no one knew he was working on credit. This is not, surely, such a strong condemnation as some commentators would have us think. Modern business is largely run on 'notional' money, and part of ordinary commercial practice is to give the impression of being always in good credit to inspire confidence in customers.

So estatly was he of his governaunce,
With his bargaynes, and with his chevisaunce.
For sothe he was a worthy man with-alle,
But sooth to seyn, I noot how men him calle.

282 *chevisaunce*: this, however, is another matter. We may translate it as 'money-lending', but it was a business euphemism, meaning vaguely 'dealing', which was used to cover the real thing. The medieval Church constantly condemned money-lending, adducing scripture to support its arguments: this was one of the reasons why Jews were associated with usury, since they were outside the Church. Very high rates of interest of up to 100 per cent could be charged, according to the urgency of the needs of the borrower.

283 *worthy*: this can mean 'worthy of respect', which the Merchant clearly is not, or what we mean by 'respectable', which he was. The ambiguity may be deliberate. The man was no better or worse than most successful businessmen of his time, or perhaps any time, but, as the next portrait suggests, Chaucer did not care for the practices he represents.

The Clerk is one of Chaucer's gentlest and most affectionate portraits, and is the more effective for being placed next to the Merchant. The Clerk is humbly dressed, badly mounted, reticent in speech and very poor. His position is not easy to define: we usually call him the Clerk because we have no modern equivalent – 'cleric', 'student', 'graduate' and 'scholar' are all possible but misleading. A clergyman is still officially called 'clerk in holy orders', which suggests the essentials. Most students who managed to get to university would, after a study of the standard subjects such as grammar and rhetoric, mathematics and astronomy, proceed to the 'queen of sciences', theology, and would probably enter at least the 'minor orders' of the Church. Many did not go further and take the steps to become priests, but found work with their skills of literacy and numeracy. The association of learning and the Church is clearer if, for instance, you look at an old Oxford college: it is built like a monastery. And if you examine that strange piece of academic headgear popularly known as a 'mortar-board', you can see that it is first cousin to the biretta worn by Roman Catholic clergy.

A CLERK ther was of Oxenford also,	Clerk.
That un-to logik hadde longe y-go.	286
As lene was his hors as is a rake,	
And he nas nat right fat, I undertake;	
But loked holwe, and ther-to soberly.	
Ful thredbar was his overest courtepy;	290
For he had geten him yet no benefyce,	
Ne was so worldly for to have offyce.	
For him was lever have at his beddes heed	
Twenty bokes, clad in blak or reed,	
Of Aristotle and his philosophye,	295
Than robes riche, or fithele, or gay sautrye.	

286 *That un-to logik hadde longe y-go*: 'he had long devoted himself to logic' – that is, to the study of the traditional skill of argument or disputation. This was an important part of academic life: debates, often public, were used to try to arrive at truths which might now be done by presenting a written thesis.

290 *courtepy*: a short (woollen) coat. His poverty would not surprise Chaucer's contemporaries. Many scholars were clever boys who had managed to scramble up an education, perhaps from a kindly parish priest or small school, and then went to Oxford or Cambridge to live as best they could, often on charity.

291 *benefyce*: 'benefice', as it is now spelt, is a 'living' as a curate or priest. To get one of any value, it was necessary to have an influential friend. The next line tells us that this was unlikely because he was an 'unworldly' man: otherwise he could have got an 'offyce', a job, for example, with a guild as an accountant, or as a landowner's secretary.

293–4 *For him ... reed*: a problem passage. The grammar strictly means 'he preferred to have ... twenty books', implying that he had them. Twenty books would cost a fortune, and the argument that he was so poor because he had spent everything on his library seems unsound. So we may assume that Chaucer meant 'he would have preferred ...'

295 *Of Aristotle and his philosophye*: 'philosophye' means 'learning', as in the degree Doctor of Philosophy. Aristotle, a Greek author of the fourth century BC who wrote on an amazingly wide range of topics, was one of the great 'authorities' in Chaucer's time. He was mostly read in Latin versions, since not many scholars then read Greek.

But al be that he was a philosophre,
Yet hadde he but litel gold in cofre;
But al that he mighte of his freendes hente,
On bokes and on lerninge he it spente,   300
And bisily gan for the soules preye
Of hem that yaf him wher-with to scoleye.
Of studie took he most cure and most hede.
Noght o word spak he more than was nede,
And that was seyd in forme and reverence,   305
And short and quik, and ful of hy sentence.
Souninge in moral vertu was his speche,
And gladly wolde he lerne, and gladly teche.

297–8   *But al be ... cofre*: this joke – perhaps a common one – cannot be translated. It refers to the 'Philosopher's Stone', a supposed chemical substance which would turn ordinary metals into gold, and which was the objective of a good deal of medieval alchemy. Though the Clerk was a philosopher in the sense of being intellectually informed, he had not found the stone that would make him rich.

301   *gan*: as quite often in Chaucer, this does not have to be translated here. A rough rule is that 'gan to' is meaningful ('began to'), but without the 'to' it is a mere auxiliary. This line introduces the concept of his piety: he could not repay his benefactors in kind, but he could pray for them, and did.

305–6   *And that ... hy sentence*: several tricky words lurk here. 'And that [the few words he spoke] was said in a seemly and respectful way, was brief but full of meaning and of high moral thought.'

307   *Souninge in moral vertu was his speche*: this line is clearly an echo of the Merchant, whose speech always tended towards profit; the Clerk's always proceeds from a moral stance, as does the story he tells.

308   *And gladly wolde he lerne, and gladly teche*: no teacher could ask for a better epitaph – he was always ready to learn and always ready to pass on his learning. Slightly comical, on his skinny horse, and with his unworldly ways, the Clerk is nevertheless to be respected, 'worthy' in the best sense, for his sincerity and integrity.

The next pilgrim is the first to represent what we should call the professional classes, and he is a very superior member of the legal fraternity. A serjeant of law was a barrister of the highest rank, one of whose duties was to act as adviser to the Crown. From this level of the hierarchy, judges were chosen. The last serjeants were created in 1873, and the last holder of the title died in 1921. In every age lawyers have been the target of much abuse and satire, perhaps because of the underlying notion that they make money out of the misfortunes of others. In Chaucer's day many men of this rank did amass substantial fortunes, and there were some areas of their practice, particularly to do with property deals, where they could succeed in pleasing their client without being over-scrupulous. The wealthy and somewhat pompous lawyer is an echo of the Merchant: both are men who have turned their wits to profit. In between comes the Clerk, who, although highly educated, has chosen poverty – this order seems to be deliberate. Possibly there is a connection with the Franklin, who follows, and of whom we learn that he had some aspirations to a title. Both men are rich, and it was becoming possible to buy your way into a higher level of society.

A SERGEANT OF THE LAWE, war and wys,	Man of Lawe.
That often hadde been at the parvys,	310
Ther was also, ful riche of excellence.	
Discreet he was, and of greet reverence:	
He semed swich, his wordes weren so wyse.	
Justyce he was ful often in assyse,	
By patente and by pleyn commissioun;	315
For his science, and for his heigh renoun	

310   *parvys*: this was probably the portico of St Paul's and the area in front of it. It was apparently used for the ceremony of creating new serjeants, and was certainly a common place for lawyers and their clients to meet. So our Serjeant is of long standing and has a large clientele.

313   *wyse*: the second reference in five lines to his wisdom, but of what sort? Worldly wise, perhaps? Note also that he *seemed* so.

314   *Justyce*: this presents a technical problem Had he been made a judge, he could no longer have taken clients. But he could have been made a temporary judge for a particular sitting (which is what 'assize' literally means) by letters 'patent' – that is, open, public – from the king. This gave him full powers, hence the 'pleyn commissioun'.

316   *science*: as usual, this means 'knowledge'.

Of fees and robes hadde he many oon.
So greet a purchasour was no-wher noon.
Al was fee simple to him in effect,
His purchasing mighte nat been infect.   320
No-wher so bisy a man as he ther nas,
And yet he semed bisier than he was.
In termes hadde he caas and domes alle,
That from the tyme of king William were falle.
Therto he coude endyte, and make a thing,   325
Ther coude no wight pinche at his wryting;
And every statut coude he pleyn by rote.
He rood but hoomly in a medlee cote
Girt with a ceint of silk, with barres smale;
Of his array telle I no lenger tale.   330

317 *robes*: robes, which were costly if of good quality, were often given in addition to fees. Full judges were entitled to robes from the king three times a year.

318–20 *So greet a purchasour ... infect*: a technical passage which causes a lot of difficulty. Most of us consult the legal profession on only two matters: when we buy a house or make a will. The sale of property, or 'conveyancing' as it is called, is still beset with enough intricacies for us to need help. The superficial meaning of the passage is that he was expert at drawing up conveyances for property deals, and when he had drawn up such a document no one could pick holes in it. There are two other suggestions: one is that 'purchasour' is to be taken literally as a buyer, and the sense is that he was a smart hand at picking up a good piece of property for himself; and 'fee simple' is a punning implication that he found it easy to make money thus. Also, many large estates were, and still are, entailed – that is to say, they could not be sold by their inheritors. A man might thus come into a large property when he would rather have money at his disposal. A clever lawyer could find ways to 'break the entail', getting round the prohibition, so that it became 'fee simple' – that is, normal, absolute possession – in which case the owner was free to sell. The larger the estate, the larger the bill.

322 *And yet he semed bisier than he was*: compare the Merchant, who concealed his debts; the Serjeant must appear to have lots of clients.

323 *In termes hadde he caas and domes alle*: a reference to what is still called case law. A barrister may quote an earlier case similar to the one before the court, and the decision given, and claim that the same decision must be granted again. 'Termes' was a way of describing the cases, which were recorded by the law term in which they fell – the legal year has four terms, the academic year has three. 'Doom' meant a judgement, hence Doomsday, the day when we are all judged. He knew every case from the time of William the Conqueror – and (l. 327) every statute as well, off by heart.

325 *endyte, and make a thing*: 'compose and draw up a deed'.

328 *hoomly*: serjeants had a legal uniform, a long unbelted robe. He is wearing a short coat with a belt, so this word perhaps means 'not in official dress', rather than plainly dressed.

A Franklin, or 'freeman', meant someone who owned property in his own right – the nearest we can get to this would be to call him a squire, but of course that word has a quite different sense in Chaucerian English. Franklins were often very prosperous, undertook public duties and offices, and were respected. They did not, however, have any aristocratic rank. Interestingly, when he comes to tell his story, the Franklin begins by intimating that he wishes his son would mix more with the nobility, and the story is itself about the nature of true aristocracy. Though he is no snob or social climber, perhaps he would have liked to feel his family might one day be ennobled. He is an attractive character, so fully drawn that there have been many attempts to make him fit a real person, but he could equally well be seen as an ideal type of country gentleman.

A FRANKELEYN was in his companye;	Frankeleyn.
Whyt was his berd, as is the dayesye.	
Of his complexioun he was sangwyn.	
Wel loved he by the morwe a sop in wyn.	
To liven in delyt was ever his wone,	335
For he was Epicurus owne sone,	
That heeld opinioun, that pleyn delyt	
Was verraily felicitee parfyt.	
An housholdere, and that a greet, was he;	
Seint Julian he was in his contree.	340
His breed, his ale, was alwey after oon;	
A bettre envyned man was no-wher noon.	
With-oute bake mete was never his hous,	
Of fish and flesh, and that so plentevous,	
It snewed in his hous of mete and drinke,	345
Of alle deyntees that men coude thinke.	
After the sondry sesons of the yeer,	
So chaunged he his mete and his soper.	
Ful many a fat partrich hadde he in mewe,	
And many a breem and many a luce in stewe.	350

333   *complexioun*: this refers to the complex mixture of four 'humours', or fluids, in the body, whose balance determined both character and appearance. In the Franklin blood (*sang* in French) is predominant, so he is ruddy, outgoing, active and cheerful. See p. 101.

334   *sop in wyn*: bread, often toasted, in a rich mixture of wine, milk and flavourings.

336–8   *For he was Epicurus … felicitee parfyt*: Epicurus, the Greek philosopher of the third century BC, had come to be associated with the idea that the only happy life was one of pleasure. In fact his followers were rather austere and sought rather to avoid pain than to practise indulgence.

340   *Seint Julian*: Julian was the patron saint of hospitality.

341   *alwey after oon*: always the same quality – that is, the best.

342   *envyned*: he had a good cellar of wine – probably a lot of it English, perhaps made from his own grapes, as he is largely self-supporting.

347–8   *After the sondry sesons … soper*: of course one's diet changed according to what was available in a period when food could not easily be preserved. But there were also rules to say what kind of diet was appropriate to the different seasons.

349   *mewe*: originally a cage for a bird. Since hawks were lodged in the stable block, the word now means buildings that are, or were, stables.

350   *luce in stewe*: fishermen will know that 'luce' is an old-fashioned word for a pike, a fish still esteemed at table in France. 'Stewe' is a catch: it's a 'fishpond'. A lot of fish was eaten by those who could afford it, as the Church forbade meat on Fridays (in memory of Good Friday) and on many other important holy days. Thus large households had their own ponds in which to fatten their fish.

Wo was his cook, but-if his sauce were
Poynaunt and sharp, and redy al his gere.
His table dormant in his halle alway
Stood redy covered al the longe day.
At sessiouns ther was he lord and sire;   355
Ful ofte tyme he was knight of the shire.
An anlas and a gipser al of silk
Heng at his girdel, whyt as morne milk.
A shirreve hadde he been, and a countour;
Was no-wher such a worthy vavasour.   360

352   *poynaunt*: medieval sauces were highly flavoured, often with fierce spices (if you could afford them). This was partly to conceal the taste of meat or fish that was stale; freshwater fish tend to be rather dull eating, too.

353–4   *His table dormant … day*: the hall was the main, common living-room of a large house. It was usual to set up tables on trestles for everyone to dine together, but he has a table 'dormant' (literally 'sleeping') – that is, a permanent table which is always set (restaurants still call a place at table a cover) – for any traveller or visitor who might drop in. There is an element of religious charity here, it seems: any passer-by could be sure of food – and always the best, too.

355   *At sessiouns ther was he lord and sire*: he acted as magistrate, or Justice of the Peace, at quarterly sessions.

356   *knight of the shire*: he represented his county in the Commons when a Parliament was summoned. He was not a knight in the military sense.

357   *An anlas and a gipser al of silk*: his dagger and silk pouch suggest wealth without too much show.

358   *morne milk*: a lost comparison. You have probably seen only bottled milk: fresh from the cow it is white, but leave it until evening and it is pale yellow.

359–60   *A shirreve … vavasour*: a 'shirreve' ('shire reeve', now 'sherrif') was a royal appointment. He was responsible for county revenues to the Crown. A 'countour' was the auditor of such accounts. 'Vavasour' was an already old-fashioned word for a country gentleman.

The Guildsmen provide an amusing and amused sketch of self-made importance. In view of the variety of trades they follow, they could not all have belonged to any of the major guilds or livery companies of London, but rather to a small 'craft' guild, so they are probably big fish only in their own small local pond.

An HABERDASSHER and a CARPENTER,	Haberdassher.
A WEBBE, a DYERE, and a TAPICER,	Carpenter.
Were with us eek, clothed in o liveree,	Webbe.
Of a solempne and greet fraternitee.	Dyere.
Ful fresh and newe hir gere apyked was;	Tapicer. 365
Hir knyves were y-chaped noght with bras,	
But al with silver, wroght ful clene and weel,	
Hir girdles and hir pouches every-deel.	
Wel semed ech of hem a fair burgeys,	
To sitten in a yeldhalle on a deys.	370
Everich, for the wisdom that he can,	
Was shaply for to been an alderman.	
For catel hadde they y-nogh and rente,	
And eek hir wyves wolde it wel assente;	
And elles certein were they to blame.	375
It is ful fair to been y-clept '*ma dame*,'	
And goon to vigilyës al bifore,	
And have a mantel royalliche y-bore.	

362   *A Webbe, a Dyere, and a Tapicer*: a 'webbe' and a 'tapicer' are respectively a weaver who makes fabric and a weaver of tapestry, then much in use as wall-hanging.

364   *Of a solempne and greet fraternitee*: the line seems ironic – they probably belonged to a small 'brotherhood' but tried to be 'solempne' ('imposing').

367   *al with silver*: the Sumptuary Laws forbade the wearing of silver-mounted knives except among the very rich. This is pretentious show.

370   *yeldhalle*: 'guildhall', a building which often did double duty as a town hall for civic functions as well as for meetings of the guild. The mayor and senior councillors – 'aldermen' – sat on a raised platform – 'deys' – on these occasions.

373   *For catel hadde they y-nogh and rente*: 'catel' and 'rente' are respectively 'property' (modern legal 'chattels') and 'income', not necessarily from land as now.

374–5   *And eek hir wyves . . . to blame*: 'And also their wives would readily agree to it, or be very much in the wrong.' An amusing glance at domestic forces driving on the husbands in their social aspirations. Wives of aldermen were given the title 'Madame' (l. 376) as a politeness rather than as a right. To have your mantle carried by pages 'royalliche' (l. 378), as if you were a queen, was the summit of pretence. Note that it was carried for show, not worn.

377   *vigilyës*: this probably refers to the 'eves' of certain religious festivals, when very devout people stayed awake all night – kept vigil – in prayer. For less pious folk, it might be a time of merry-making, like a modern Christmas Eve. The guilds themselves kept certain festivals – for their patron saints, for instance – and this may refer to social gatherings the evening before such events.

The Cook is the shortest portrait, if we exclude those characters who are merely named. His chief interest to us lies in the insight which he gives us into the diet of the period. The one personal detail is repulsive – perhaps because Chaucer intended him to tell a repulsive story. In fact it promises to be so filthy that we are not surprised to find it was left unfinished.

> A COOK they hadde with hem for the nones,   Cook.
> To boille the chiknes with the mary-bones,   380
> And poudre-marchant tart, and galingale.
> Wel coude he knowe a draughte of London ale.
> He coude roste, and sethe, and broille, and frye,
> Maken mortreux, and wel bake a pye.
> But greet harm was it, as it thoughte me,   385
> That on his shine a mormal hadde he;
> For blankmanger, that made he with the beste.

379 *with hem for the nones*: 'with hem' appears to mean 'with the
Guildsmen' rather than 'with all the pilgrims', and he has been brought
along 'for the nones', an expression often used with little meaning, but
here in the sense of 'for the occasion' – they must have wished to make
a big impression if they brought their own cook. No one else did.

380–81 *To boille ... galingale*: the passage abounds in technical words.
'Mary-bones' ('marrow-bones') remind us of the love of fat. 'Poudre-
marchant tart' is *not* a tart, but a sharp, spiced sauce-powder, rather
like curry powder. 'Galingale' was a sweeter flavouring prepared from
a root. 'Mortreux' (note the French plural) were very thick soups or
stews, for which the meat had been tenderized by pounding in a mortar.
And his 'blankmanger' was not the insipid wobbly sweet of today, but
a rich mixture of white sauce, minced chicken and flavourings. The
emphasis on heavy flavouring has been explained in reference to the
Franklin's cook.

382 *coude he knowe*: 'he easily recognized' London ale, which was
reputed to be strong. He turns out to be a drunkard.

386 *mormal*: this detail, much nastier because it is mentioned at the same
time as food, refers to an open ulcer. Suggestions that it is syphilitic
should be treated cautiously, as the disease probably did not reach
Europe until a century later. Chronic varicose ulcers are hard to heal
even today.

The Shipman, or Sailor, is treated almost as though he were a different species, as indeed he was. Life at sea was dangerous and often short. It was a traditional occupation for men of the West Country as it is to this day. It is as well that, when he comes to tell his story, Chaucer did not try to write it in the dialect of the West Country, which would have been a foreign language to his London hearers.

The portrait is of a man who lived a hard and dangerous life, which made him a hard and, in his own business, merciless man. It is interesting that the relentless energies of scholars have managed to suggest a real person as being the origin even of this portrait – it hardly helps us to know that there was someone called John Hawley who may have inspired it.

A SHIPMAN was ther, woning fer by weste: Shipman.
Four aught I woot, he was of Dertemouthe.
He rood up-on a rouncy, as he couthe,   390
In a gowne of falding to the knee.
A daggere hanging on a laas hadde he
Aboute his nekke under his arm adoun.
The hote somer had maad his hewe al broun;
And, certeinly, he was a good felawe.   395
Ful many a draughte of wyn had he y-drawe
From Burdeux-ward, whyl that the chapman sleep.
Of nyce conscience took he no keep.
If that he faught, and hadde the hyer hond,
By water he sente hem hoom to every lond.   400

389   *For aught I woot*: this shows how remote some parts of England were to a Londoner – Chaucer speaks of Dartmouth as if it were Timbuktoo. Elsewhere he refers to 'the North' as a foreign territory.

390   *He rood up-on a rouncy, as he couthe*: 'he rode a nag as well as he could' – a traditional joke, which is not yet dead, that a sailor is a poor horseman. A 'rouncy' can be found by admirers of Don Quixote in *Rosin*ante, literally 'a nag (before he became a knight's charger)'. Probably the horse was hired at the Tabard and was a wretched hack. The inn had big stables, as we are later told.

392   *laas*: the seaman's 'lanyard' suggests itself here as the right word.

396–7   *Ful many a draughte ... sleep*: much ink has been spilt on this passage. He has carried many cargoes of wine from Bordeaux while the merchants, who travelled with it, slept on his ship. But a 'draughte' can also mean a drink, and there were various ways of drawing off wine from casks for your own drinking (while the buyer slept) and replacing it with water, and this may be intended. The custom continued amongst smugglers into the nineteenth century – Thomas Hardy describes it well in his *Wessex Tales*.

398   *nyce*: this has the sense of 'fastidious, finicky', still retained in 'that's a nice point' in a debate.

399–400   *If that he faught ... lond*: piracy has already been mentioned. If the Shipman got involved in a fight and won, he sent his prisoners home, wherever they lived, by sea – that is, he made them walk the plank or just tipped them overboard.

But of his craft to rekene wel his tydes,
His stremes and his daungers him bisydes,
His herberwe and his mone, his lodemenage,
Ther nas noon swich from Hulle to Cartage.
Hardy he was, and wys to undertake;   405
With many a tempest hadde his berd been shake.
He knew wel alle the havenes, as they were,
From Gootlond to the cape of Finistere,
And every cryke in Britayne and in Spayne;
His barge y-cleped was the Maudelayne.   410

401–3 *But of his craft ... lodemenage*: there are many technical terms here. Tides and currents were dangerous to vessels having only the wind to propel them. Knowing safe anchorages ('herberwe') was as important as the phases of the moon, which affects the tides, and the inshore skill of the pilot ('lodemenage'). Again, a knowledge of safe harbours ('havenes', l. 407) was very important for those in sailing-ships, since they might need to put into harbour at short notice if the winds were to turn against them or a storm to blow up; likewise, a knowledge of creeks ('cryke', l. 409).

404 *Cartage*: the ruins of ancient Carthage, near to modern Tunis, may have served as a landmark, but it seems more likely that the medieval sailor, who liked to hug the coast where he could, means Cartagena in Spain.

408 *From Gootlond to the cape of Finistere*: Gotland on the Baltic was an important centre of trade. Cap Finisterre, the tip of Spain, gives us a notion of the Shipman's range. He knew the whole of the coast of Western Europe.

409 *Britayne*: this is easy to misread. He refers to Brittany, which, with its dangerous western coast, was the subject of at least one of the tales, the Franklin's. Chaucer seems to have known the district personally.

410 *Maudelayne*: the spelling indicates the medieval pronunciation of Magdalene, which is still in use at the colleges named after St Mary Magdalene at Oxford and Cambridge. Since, in the medieval mind, she was thought of as a reformed prostitute, it is perhaps a slightly suggestive, or blasphemous, name for a ship, depending on your point of view. The sailor, who had not a fastidious conscience, perhaps thought of her name as, say, 'The Saucy Jane' or something of the kind.

The portrait of the Doctor, a very full one, is a surprise to most modern readers, who do not expect their medical advisers to be experts in astrology or to be basing their practice on writers of the fourth century BC, or indeed upon an authority (Aesculapius) who left no written records at all and was probably mythical. It is necessary to emphasize two points here. First, medieval people believed implicitly in the influence of the stars, which governed not only our characters and destinies, but the different parts of our bodies. A doctor thus had to know how to calculate the most suitable time to administer a particular medicine, according to the position of the relevant planets. Second, the huge list of authors with which the Doctor is familiar is probably not as satirical as some commentators suggest: as has been said elsewhere, in the Middle Ages there was great respect for 'authority' – if it was in Aristotle, it was true. In fact the Doctor is not so out of date as it may seem, since his reading ranges from about 400 BC to a man who died when Chaucer was twenty-one. It seems likely that he was intended to be thought of as a good physician, but, of course, an expensive one. In those times no common man consulted a doctor. He made his money from the rich. It is also true that he made that money from the misfortunes of others, just like the Serjeant, and perhaps it is that underlying thought that colours this portrait – line 442, which tells us he was rich because he saved up all the money he made when there was an outbreak of plague, is chilling to think about.

> With us ther was a DOCTOUR OF PHISYK,   Doctour.
> In al this world ne was ther noon him lyk
> To speke of phisik and of surgerye;
> For he was grounded in astronomye.
> He kepte his pacient a ful greet del   415
> In houres, by his magik naturel.
> Wel coude he fortunen the ascendent
> Of his images for his pacient.

413 *To speke of*: 'if you are talking about'.

414–18 *For he was grounded ... pacient*: he had a sound knowledge of astrology, or 'magik naturel'. This was regarded as a science, and, as it was based upon observation of the heavens, was distinct from 'black' magic, which depended on communication with evil spirits. The Doctor's method was to observe ('kepe') his patient carefully as the planets moved into different relationships with one another. He well knew how to determine the best time to administer a remedy according to the dominant planet.

418 *images*: this means what it says. Amongst other remedies, images either of a zodiacal sign or the afflicted part were made to be worn or applied, as some people still wear a copper bangle in the belief that it will cure arthritis. Such images had to be made at the correct astrological time. The subject is far more complex than useful to our understanding of Chaucer, and only the outline of the theory is needed. Each part of the body was governed by a zodiacal sign – if you suffered from stomach ache or heart attacks, Leo was the sign to watch, for example – and, in fact, a knowledge of astronomy was considered essential to the proper practice of medicine, since you diagnosed a person's temperament, or 'complexion', from the conjunction of planets at his birth; the bodily location of the complaint also had its appropriate sign, and the twenty-four hours of the day were divided into four periods, each of which was related to a bodily fluid. These are mentioned under their attributes in l. 420.

He knew the cause of everich maladye,
Were it of hoot or cold, or moiste, or drye,   420
And where engendred, and of what humour;
He was a verrey parfit practisour.
The cause y-knowe, and of his harm the rote,
Anon he yaf the seke man his bote.
Ful redy hadde he his apothecaries,   425
To sende him drogges and his letuaries,
For ech of hem made other for to winne;
Hir frendschipe nas nat newe to biginne.

420   *hoot or cold, or moiste, or drye*: the four fluids in the body, blood,
yellow bile or choler, black bile or choler, and phlegm, which were the
foundations of a man's personality (sanguine, choleric, melancholy
and phlegmatic, words we still use) were also the foundation of medical
theory. An excessive amount of any of these fluids led to illness. This
explains the extraordinary amount of blood-letting that went on, since
in so many illnesses the patient is hot, suggesting that the blood is
heated, so that it was necessary to draw some off – but not between
midnight and six in the morning, as this section of the day was very
dangerous to this humour. Blood was hot and moist, choler was hot
and dry, black bile was cold and dry, phlegm was cold and moist. The
line essentially means that he knew the origin of every illness, from
whatever combination of humours it arose, and in what part of the
body it originated.

It is easy to scoff at this strange rigmarole, and even to think Chaucer
was making fun too. Yet horoscopes still appear in many popular
magazines, and innumerable birth signs are sold and worn to this day.
Modern medicine would agree that an imbalance of glandular secre-
tions upsets our whole metabolism and even affects our behaviour: the
menopausal shop-lifter is a frequently cited example, and we have all
lived through an unpredictable adolescence.

422   *a verrey parfit practisour*: again we have an echo of Chaucer's
famous line about the Knight. It is difficult to argue that it is satirical
here: the Doctor is, by the criteria of the time, good at his job.

424   *bote*: 'appropriate remedy'. The previous line suggests correctly that
a physician's greatest skill lies in diagnosis.

425–8   *Ful redy ... to biginne*: the charge that doctors and pharmacists
worked hand in glove was a common one, and probably true. Charges
are still made that some doctors too freely prescribe expensive medicines when cheaper varieties are available.

Wel knew he the olde Esculapius,
And Deiscorides, and eek Rufus,   430
Old Ypocras, Haly, and Galien;
Serapion, Razis, and Avicen;
Averrois, Damascien, and Constantyn;
Bernard, and Gatesden, and Gilbertyn.
Of his diete mesurable was he,   435
For it was of no superfluitee,
But of greet norissing and digestible.
His studie was but litel on the Bible.
In sangwin and in pers he clad was al,
Lyned with taffata and with sendal;   440
And yet he was but esy of dispence;
He kepte that he wan in pestilence.
For gold in phisik is a cordial,
Therfore he lovede gold in special.

429–34 *Wel knew he ... and Gilbertyn*: this passage appals many readers when first they come to it. Most editions have notes, often too extensive to be helpful, but useful in giving the modern spellings. We have probably heard of the Hippocratic Oath, which some medical faculties are still said to regard as binding on newly qualified doctors, so once 'Ypocras' is turned into 'Hippocrates' we feel the ground is more familiar. Basically, Chaucer's list, not always in a very clear order, covers three areas of medical authority: that of the Greeks of antiquity, of whom Hippocrates remains the best-known and Aesculapius is to be found in books of legends rather than medical texts; then the great Arab writers, whose interest in medicine, astrology and mathematics can be traced in such Arabic words as 'alkaline', 'zenith' and 'algebra'; and lastly a group of more nearly contemporary authors, the Englishmen Gilbert and John of Gaddesden, and the Scots Bernard Gordon. There is much dispute about the significance of this list, the fact that the writers are not in any strict order, that one of them (Aesculapius) did not exist and so on. Chaucer probably lifted the whole lot from one of the medieval equivalents of an encyclopedia, though several of the authors may have been known to him since they were not specifically writers on medicine, but rather commentators on a wide range of learned topics. The catalogue represents the medieval respect for 'authority' and, if we take it at its face value, it shows the Doctor as very well informed. The supposed disorder of the list may be no more than the result of having to fit some difficult names into a pattern of verse.

438 *His studie was but litel on the Bible*: a traditional joke – 'Where there are three doctors, two are atheists.'

439–40 *In sangwin ... with sendal*: his wealth is shown in his dress, with its lining of expensive silks, its blue-grey fur and bright red colour. It is perhaps intentional that the word 'sangwin' is used for the latter colour, as it was also the name of a temperament and part of his professional vocabulary.

442 *pestilence*: this refers to the periodic outbreaks of plague which were a feature of life in England for nearly four centuries. The medical profession was doubtless much in demand then, but their remedies were entirely useless because the nature of the disease was not understood at all.

443–4 *For gold ... in special*: 'cordial' is a tonic or stimulant (the root of the word is the French for 'heart'). Gold was used in medicine, and still is in injections for some forms of rheumatism. It was a costly specific, so profitable. Hence the last line of the portrait – he found gold a particularly good pick-me-up: he was a mercenary man.

In the Wife of Bath it is tempting to see an early feminist. She is a bold, outspoken woman, already elderly for those times, much married and the only female character, apart from the Prioress, to be described in detail. She tells a story whose moral *appears* to be that women, in their affairs with men, prefer above all things to be in charge. Yet she herself is capable of falling for a husband because he is handsome, even though he treats her badly. In her enormous introduction to her tale – it is almost exactly as long as *The Prologue* itself – she explains how she married old men, got them to make over their money to her and then wore them out by a mixture of nagging and sexual demands. She is thus quite rich and independent. In addition, she has a trade which was, at that time, largely practised by women. The woollen industry has already been referred to as a major one. Much of it was carried out in the home. This explains why she has been prosperous enough to travel so widely – no one but the Knight seems to have got about as much as she. She obviously loves travel for the society it provides her with.

A good WYF was ther of bisyde BATHE,	Wyf of Bathe.
But she was som-del deef, and that was scathe.	446
Of clooth-making she hadde swiche an haunt,	
She passed hem of Ypres and of Gaunt.	
In al the parisshe wyf ne was ther noon	
That to the offring bifore hir sholde goon;	450
And if ther dide, certeyn, so wrooth was she,	
That she was out of alle charitee.	
Hir coverchiefs ful fyne were of ground;	
I dorste swere they weyeden ten pound	
That on a Sonday were upon hir heed.	455
Hir hosen weren of fyn scarlet reed,	
Ful streite y-teyd, and shoos ful moiste and newe.	
Bold was hir face, and fair, and reed of hewe.	

445   *A good Wyf was ther of bisyde Bathe*: 'wyf' implied any adult woman. 'Bisyde' could simply mean outside the civic limits. Chaucer may have known Bath, as it would lie on his route to North Petherton of which he was first Deputy, later sole Forester.

446   *But she was som-del deef, and that was scathe*: her slight deafness was the result of a blow received in a matrimonial dispute, as she later tells us. That it was a pity may suggest that she unfortunately talked more than she listened, or perhaps talked very loudly, as deaf people sometimes do.

448   *Ypres and of Gaunt*: we have previously referred to the presence of Flemish weavers in England. They may have come from Ypres and Ghent to work in this country.

450   *offring*: probably not of money, but going up to the altar with an offering of bread and wine to be used in the communion.

452   *That she was out of alle charitee*: almost an echo of words used at the Eucharist to this day, to the effect that anyone not in love and charity with their neighbour is excluded.

453–5   *Hir coverchiefs ... heed*: the description of her elaborate Sunday headgear is amusing and not merely a quaint custom of the past. Very big hats bedecked with flowers and fruit were very common until recent times, as photographs of workers on holiday earlier this century show.

456–7   *Hir hosen ... moiste and newe*: we notice again the expensive footwear. We also notice the shameless scarlet of the stockings, as bold as they were expensive. That she wore her stockings tight to the leg ('y-teyd' with garters) we should not notice, as she should have kept them concealed.

458   *Bold was hir face, and fair, and reed of hewe*: as she herself later explains, she was born under a combination of Mars and Venus, which would make her bold-featured and ruddy (Mars) and handsome (Venus).

She was a worthy womman al hir lyve,
Housbondes at chirche-dore she hadde fyve, 460
Withouten other companye in youthe;
But therof nedeth nat to speke as nouthe.
And thryes hadde she been at Jerusalem;
She hadde passed many a straunge streem;
At Rome she hadde been, and at Boloigne, 465
In Galice at seint Jame, and at Coloigne.

460 *Housbondes at chirche-dore she hadde fyve*: the church disapproved of remarriage, an attitude not quite extinct in the Roman Church to this day; and she has married many times, and is, she says, looking out again. Much of her preamble to her story is taken up with a riotous account of her matrimonial experience – and a very powerful denunciation of the Church in its attitude to marriage and to sexual enjoyment. In those days marriages did take place in the door or porch of the church, partly as the ceremony was supposed to be public, partly because the couple, whose thoughts might well have been on matters not strictly religious, were not allowed to enter the sacred building until they were truly married, when they could take Nuptial Mass together as man and wife.

463–4 *And thryes ... straunge streem*: here begins the account of her remarkable travels. A journey without major hitches to Jerusalem, the most important pilgrimage a Christian could make, took a year. She must have been both a tough traveller and a compulsive one to make this passage three times. Crossing 'straunge streems' ('foreign rivers') would be the least of her perils.

465–6 *At Rome ... at Coloigne*: besides the great journey to Jerusalem, she seems to have got herself to most of the more famous European shrines. Rome, of course, is still a major centre for the pious, and then boasted even more relics and hallowed places than are today officially recognized. Bologna had its pilgrim attractions, but so did Boulogne in the Church of Our Lady, and most commentators favour this reading – it is, in any case, nearer to the accepted form of the name. There was a very important shrine of Saint James of Compostella, in Galicia, so she has been to Spain. Cologne had the honour of being the supposed resting-place of the Wise Men of the Epiphany story, and also – the object of a good deal of scandalous mockery – the bones of no less than eleven thousand virgins who had been martyred for the Christian faith. Charles Reade gives a half-humorous explanation that there were only two, but one was called Onesimilla, or little Onesima, and someone who did not recognize the odd Greek name turned it into corrupt Latin, *undecim mille*, eleven thousand. It is instructive as well as amusing to read the tirade against medieval religious credulity which occupies much of Chapter 72 of Reade's *The Cloister and the Hearth*. It makes the success of tricksters like the Pardoner much easier to understand.

She coude muche of wandring by the weye.
Gat-tothed was she, soothly for to seye.
Up-on an amblere esily she sat,
Y-wimpled wel, and on hir heed an hat   470
As brood as is a bokeler or a targe;
A foot-mantel aboute hir hipes large,
And on hir feet a paire of spores sharpe.
In felawschip wel coude she laughe and carpe.
Of remedyes of love she knew per-chaunce,   475
For she coude of that art the olde daunce.

468　*Gat-tothed*: it is instructive to look at the learned wrangling that
'gat-tothed' has inspired. Either her teeth are widely spaced, which
seems likely as this is a physical description, or she is goat-toothed –
that is, has an appetite for sex (the goat being a common sexual image)
– as we might say she had a sweet tooth. What is certain is that either
reading means she was lustful, which indeed she was; but, to complicate
the problem, such teeth were held to denote someone who travelled
widely – as she did.

469　*amblere*: a horse with an easy pace. It is sometimes used for the
artificial step in which hind and foreleg on the same side move together,
which is a comfortable step for someone riding sidesaddle, but as she
wears a pair of spurs and sidesaddle riders use only one, this seems
improbable. Most medieval women who rode still sat astride, but the
sharp spurs ('spores sharpe', l. 473) – it is taken for granted that all the
men wore them, so they are never mentioned – surely imply something
mannish and bold in her.

474　*In felawschip wel coude she laughe and carpe*: like the Prioress, but
in a much less decorous way, she is good company – she also wears a
wimple ('y-wimpled', l. 470). 'Carpe' is not to criticize, but to chatter
in a rather boastful way.

475　*remedyes of love*: there was a text called the *Remedies of Love*, a
supplement to Ovid's better-known *Art of Love*, a popular handbook
of seduction that is still fun to read. She might have known of it because,
as she later explains, one of her husbands was a scholar and used to
read scandalous stuff aloud, and because looking for new lovers was
a remedy suggested by Ovid.

476　*For she coude of that art the olde daunce*: beyond translation – 'She
knew all the tricks of that old trade'?

The Parson – a very extended portrait – is the only representative of the Church for whom Chaucer clearly felt admiration. In contrast to the many corrupt ecclesiastical folk, of whom the worst are yet to come, the simple village priest is held up as the example of the true Christian who follows the precepts of his Master, as the friars were supposed to, and embodies in himself and his own actions the basic charity and humility of the genuine believer. Chaucer intended this modest, poorly paid man to have the honour of finishing the grand scheme of 120 tales, and had actually written his story for him. It is a sermon on the seven deadly sins – those that condemned the soul to hell – and, if rather strange to modern ears, it is nevertheless a practical piece of preaching, for each sin is clearly identified, its causes are explained and remedies proposed. It remains open to question, as it does with the Knight, whether this portrait is meant to be a real person or an idealization of all that is best in the Church.

A good man was ther of religioun,	Persoun.
And was a povre PERSOUN of a toun;	
But riche he was of holy thoght and werk.	
He was also a lerned man, a clerk,	480
That Cristes gospel trewely wolde preche;	
His parisshens devoutly wolde he teche.	
Benigne he was, and wonder diligent,	
And in adversitee ful pacient;	
And swich he was y-preved ofte sythes.	485
Ful looth were him to cursen for his tythes,	
But rather wolde he yeven, out of doute,	
Un-to his povre parisshens aboute	
Of his offring, and eek of his substaunce.	
He coude in litel thing han suffisaunce.	490

478 *Persoun of a town*: a small village or township is indicated, and he is the parish priest, whose income is derived from tithes – that is, tenths of the produce of his parishioners. Many such men, in remote, rural areas, were very poor indeed. The more important tithes, such as grain and fodder, were taken by the landlord and lost to the priest.

480 *clerk*: always a difficult word, as we have seen; perhaps here it implies a graduate. Many scholars were poor, like the Clerk himself. The Parson preaches quite an erudite sermon.

485 *y-preved*: the past form of the verb 'to prove', which is also 'to probe' meaning 'to test'. In Chaucer the word carries something of both senses. His patience in adversity had often been put to the test.

486 *cursen*: if a man did not pay his tenths, he could be excommunicated – that is, prevented from taking the sacraments. This was serious, since it might mean if he fell ill he would be denied the last rites. The 'curse' was redeemed by paying a fine, but if that were unpaid for forty days the man was liable to imprisonment. In corrupt hands, the power to excommunicate was an easy way of raising money. This the Parson would never do.

489 *offring, and eek of his substaunce*: 'offring' and 'substaunce' refer, in reverse order, to the Parson's own property, or capital, which was probably very little, and to the offerings made by the parishioners. Traditionally, the 'collection' in church at Easter still goes to the priest.

Wyd was his parisshe, and houses fer a-sonder,
But he ne lafte nat, for reyn ne thonder,
In siknes nor in meschief, to visyte
The ferreste in his parisshe, muche and lyte,
Up-on his feet, and in his hand a staf.   495
This noble ensample to his sheep he yaf,
That first he wroghte, and afterward he taughte;
Out of the gospel he tho wordes caughte;
And this figure he added eek ther-to,
That if gold ruste, what shal iren do?   500
For if a preest be foul, on whom we truste,
No wonder is a lewed man to ruste;
And shame it is, if a preest take keep,
A shiten shepherde and a clene sheep.
Wel oghte a preest ensample for to yive,   505
By his clennesse, how that his sheep shold live.
He sette nat his benefice to hyre,
And leet his sheep encombred in the myre,

493   *meschief*: 'misfortune', 'trouble'. He took his responsibility to visit
the sick or troubled parishioners very seriously, though his parish was
a widely scattered one.

495   *Up-on his feet*: here he is following the example of the first apostles,
who went out into the world simply dressed and equipped, on their own
two feet.

496   *his sheep*: traditional imagery for clergy and people, derived from
the story of the good shepherd in St John, Chapter 10. It had more force
in times when a shepherd literally lived with his flock on the grazing-
grounds.

497   *wroghte*: the old irregular past tense of 'work', which survives in
'wrought iron'. The Parson acted first, then drew lessons from the act.
As Chaucer later says, 'The words must be related to the actions'
(l. 742).

498   *the gospel*: probably Matthew 5:19 – 'whosoever shall *do and teach*
... shall be called great in the kingdom of heaven'.

499   *figure*: 'figure of speech', 'metaphor'.

502   *lewed*: the meaning of this word has gone down in the world, and
now implies a crude vulgarity. In Chaucer it usually means 'uneducated', 'ignorant', and reminds us that the priest was often the only
educated man in a community, and thus looked up to not only as a
spiritual leader but as a man of learning. Literacy and the Church were
closely linked, as we see in the case of the Clerk.

503–4   *And shame it is ... clene sheep*: 'And it is shameful, if a priest
thinks about it, that the shepherd should be foul and the sheep clean.'
Chaucer uses a blunt enough word for 'foul' here – an accurate one,
too: untended sheep get themselves very filthy and matted.

507   *He sette nat his benefice to hyre*: it was quite common to get a really
poor curate in to carry out parish duties for a tiny part of the true
income. Many clergymen held a whole series of livings and 'hired' them
out in this way.

113

> And ran to London, un-to sëynt Poules,
> To seken him a chaunterie for soules, 510
> Or with a bretherhed to been withholde;
> But dwelte at hoom, and kepte wel his folde,
> So that the wolf ne made it nat miscarie;
> He was a shepherde and no mercenarie.
> And though he holy were, and vertuous, 515
> He was to sinful man nat despitous,
> Ne of his speche daungerous ne digne,
> But in his teching discreet and benigne.
> To drawen folk to heven by fairnesse
> By good ensample, was his bisinesse: 520
> But it were any persone obstinat,
> What-so he were, of heigh or lowe estat,
> Him wolde he snibben sharply for the nones.
> A bettre preest, I trowe that nowher noon is.
> He wayted after no pompe and reverence, 525
> Ne maked him a spyced conscience,
> But Cristes lore, and his apostles twelve,
> He taughte, and first he folwed it him-selve.

509–10   *And ran to London ... chaunterie for soules*: 'chaunterie' was a 'chantry', a tiny chapel, of which there were over thirty inside St Paul's. The cathedral was destroyed later in the Great Fire, but in many old cathedrals such chapels can be found – just big enough to say Mass in. Wealthy families or guilds sometimes endowed such a chapel, and left a sum to have Masses said there regularly for the souls of dead members. Since a Low Mass can be pattered off in twenty minutes or less, such a post was a sinecure.

511   *a bretherhed*: 'a guild'. Prosperous ones might have their own chaplain, another job that carried minimal duties with security.

517   *daungerous ne digne*: 'neither forbidding nor superior'.

520   *bisinesse*: used in its basic sense. His whole concern, that which he most busied himself about, was to attract souls to heaven by gentle methods and by his own example.

522   *of heigh or lowe estat*: this is not a mere phrase. The priest, in his office, fears no man, whatever his rank, and reproves where it is necessary.

523   *for the nones*: a good example of this stop-gap phrase being used in its proper sense, and so requiring to be translated. He would reprove such a man sharply on that occasion – implying that once it was done, he would revert to his normal quiet and kindly manner.

525   *wayted after*: he did not expect any special ceremony or respect to be shown to him.

526   *spyced conscience*: this phrase has caused much speculation, though the basic sense must surely be that he had strict rules for himself. Most of us make small adjustments in our moral code and do not consider that principles which we expect others to follow should apply unreservedly to us. Our conscience is thus corrupt, or tainted. In medieval times, spices were greatly valued to hide the taste of meat that was rather high. Reversing the image, we can say that he never tried to hide from his own conscience.

527   *lore*: 'teaching' or 'doctrine'. That of Christ and his Apostles is, of course, to be found in the Gospels and Acts.

528   *He taughte, and first he folwed it him-selve*: this line recapitulates the main theme of the whole portrait. He did not expect others to do what he was not first prepared to do himself.

The Parson probably came from a poor home, but was clever enough to scrape up a little Latin and struggle his way to ordination: it is not surprising that the Ploughman should be his brother, since the two exemplify all that is best in the Christian life between them, one as a priest, the other as a layman. The Ploughman, having a special skill, and possibly a little land of his own, had a little more independence than most land-workers, and so he could go on pilgrimage. He is mentioned in the same breath as the remaining pilgrims (ll. 542–4), and an odd contrast they make: the Reeve and the Miller, who tell two stories of gross impropriety; the disgusting, corrupt Summoner and Pardoner; the sharp-bargaining Manciple; and Chaucer himself, who is not described until he tells a story (he claims to be a poor narrator, begins an awful poem in a verse-form that jingles along like 'Mary had a little lamb', is stopped by the Host, says the only other thing he knows is a little thing in prose, and tells a long, moral and utterly boring story about Melibeus).

With him ther was a PLOWMAN, was his brother,	Plowman.
That hadde y-lad of dong ful many a fother,	530
A trewe swinker and a good was he,	
Livinge in pees and parfit charitee.	
God loved he best with al his hole herte	
At alle tymes, thogh him gamed or smerte,	
And thanne his neighebour right as him-selve.	535
He wolde thresshe, and ther-to dyke and delve,	

530 *That hadde y-lad of dong ful many a fother*: 'who had carted many a load of manure'. The verb 'to lead' is still used in country districts, because when a cart is laden – and dung is a very heavy load indeed – the carter walks at the horse's head and leads it instead of sitting on the cart and driving. This is the first of the many jobs the Ploughman knows how to do, besides his own special skill. Most of them are well described as 'swink' – very heavy tasks. Ploughing itself, in pre-mechanized days, was very tiring to man and beast, and needed great patience too.

534 *thogh him gamed or smerte*: another example of an impersonal. We should say: 'whether he was happy or in trouble'.

535 *And thanne his neighebour right as him-selve*: an echo of the second of the two great commandments, on which all the others rest; the first – to love God – has already been given (l. 533). He loves his neighbour in a highly practical way, as did the Good Samaritan, whose story illustrates the rule.

536 *He wolde thresshe, and ther-to dyke and delve*: threshing is hard work, and in those times, using flails, it was very hard indeed. We still hear 'dyke' for 'ditch' and the clearing of ditches, clogged up with mud and overgrown with briars, was also arduous toil. To 'delve' is to 'dig', and probably goes with dyke – new ditches had to be dug out, old ones dug clear.

For Cristes sake, for every povre wight,
Withouten hyre, if it lay in his might.
His tythes payed he ful faire and wel,
Bothe of his propre swink and his catel.   540
In a tabard he rood upon a mere.
    Ther was also a Reve and a Millere,
A Somnour and a Pardoner also,
A Maunciple, and my-self; ther were namo.

539 *His tythes payed he ful faire and wel*: most people probably paid
their tithes grudgingly, and chose the poorest tenth to give to the
Church. There was an old joke that when a sow had a litter, the runt,
or smallest piglet, was the tithe pig. The Ploughman, however, pays up
handsomely.

540 *Bothe of his propre swink and his catel*: he also paid partly in kind.
'His propre swink' is his own labour, 'proper' here being used as it still
is in French; 'catel' is the modern legal term 'chattels', meaning
property.

541 *In a tabard he rood upon a mere*: a tabard was a sleeveless jacket,
worn loose. While we associate it with the splendid state garments worn
by heralds, it was also a very humble affair, not unlike a smock. The
reference to his riding a mare is also indicative of humility. Men of
any standing rode a stallion or gelding. He is not too proud to appear
in his working coat, and was very probably riding one of his own
farm-horses.

542 *Ther was also ... namo*: after this pair of brothers – brothers in
Christ as well as in blood – who represent all that is best in clergy and
laity, there is a gaggle of men who would instantly be recognized as a
very different sort. Reeves and summoners were hated, millers were
swindlers, pardoners were notorious con-men, manciples – we can only
suggest 'caterer' as an alternative word – had at least to be smart buyers.
Chaucer himself remains the observer, undescribed.

Millers were unpopular because they had a monopoly – a man with corn to grind had to take it to the local mill – and because they could very easily swindle, since it was hard, without exact weighing devices, to know how much flour your corn would make, or how much he had taken as his 'toll'. This man is presented in a brutish way – animal imagery abounds – and as being thoroughly coarse-grained. He does indeed tell a very rude story, but it is extremely well told. It is, in fact, the second of the tales, since the drunken Miller forces the Host to let him speak immediately after the Knight has ended. As we shall see, he seems to have a permanent quarrel with the Reeve, and his story is directed against an elderly carpenter: the Reeve is not young, and was brought up to be a carpenter.

The MILLER was a stout carl, for the nones,	Miller.
Ful big he was of braun, and eek of bones;	546
That proved wel, for over-al ther he cam,	
At wrastling he wolde have alwey the ram.	
He was short-sholdred, brood, a thikke knarre,	
Ther nas no dore that he nolde heve of harre,	550
Or breke it, at a renning, with his heed.	
His berd as any sowe or fox was reed,	
And ther-to brood, as though it were a spade.	
Up-on the cop right of his nose he hade	
A werte, and ther-on stood a tuft of heres,	555
Reed as the bristles of a sowes eres;	
His nose-thirles blake were and wyde.	
A swerd and bokeler bar he by his syde;	

545   *carl*: 'churl' the word suggests he was low-bred, vulgar.

547–8   *That proved wel ... the ram*: 'that proved wel' here means 'that had been well tested', because he always took the first prize in wrestling. There were traditional prizes at country fairs for some contests – a ram was suitable for wrestling, and well into the present century such fairs featured 'skittling for a pig', a useful prize to a cottager.

549   *He was short-sholdred, brood, a thikke knarre*: a difficult line to adequately translate. The sense is clearly that he was very thick-set and probably bull-necked.

550   *dore*: the 'dore' referred to might well be a barn door. These were big enough to admit loaded carts, and at harvest-time it might have been quicker and given more space to lift them off their simple peg-and-ring hinges, in which case the brute strength of the Miller would have come in handy.

551   *Or breke it, at a renning, with his heed*: why he should break a door down or split it open by charging at it head-on is not clear. It sounds like a drunken wager, and he later proves to be a drunkard.

552–7   *His berd ... wyde*: note the animal imagery, together with his hairiness and the flattened, ape-like nostrils.

558   *bokeler*: 'buckler' – a small, round shield, easily carried in this way.

His mouth as greet was as a greet forneys.
He was a janglere and a goliardeys,   560
And that was most of sinne and harlotryes.
Wel coude he stelen corn, and tollen thryes;
And yet he hadde a thombe of gold, pardee.
A whyt cote and a blew hood wered he.
A baggepype wel coude he blowe and sowne,   565
And ther-with-al he broghte us out of towne.

559   *forneys*: probably better understood as 'oven' than 'furnace' – the gaping entrance of a medieval bread-oven, for instance, suggests the big-mouth that the Miller is.

560–61   *He was a janglere ... harlotryes*: Chaucer tells us that he was an obscene chatterer, and his subject was mostly sinful indecency. This is indeed the case, for he tells a very rude story, but tells it very well, perhaps because practice had given him some skill in the matter.

562   *Wel coude he stelen corn, and tollen thryes*: this line explains the entire, hostile portrait. Millers could easily swindle their customers and take thrice the amount that was their due.

563   *And yet he hadde a thombe of gold, pardee*: much dispute has been aroused about this line, which presumably rests on the proverb 'An honest miller has a thumb of gold', which is like saying you will meet an honest miller in a month of Sundays. It has been suggested that his thumb was 'golden' because he used it to test samples of grain – as is indeed done – and this was an important skill; or else that it means he was relatively honest, compared with most millers. The stumbling-block is the word 'yet', suggesting that *though* he stole so much he nevertheless had a 'golden thumb'.

565   *A baggepype wel coude he blowe and sowne*: bagpipes were common peasant instruments, with no special Scottish association. The skill of piping lies partly in controlling the air supply from the bag and partly in playing the tune on the chanter, so both the verbs here – 'blow and sound', or 'play' – have meaning. The bagpipe was also a well-recognized symbol of lust, especially in paintings, because of its phallic appearance, and the tumescence that results from blowing it.

566   *And ther-with-al he broghte us out of towne*: an innocent line that conceals an important fact. He heads the company with his instrument – but the Reeve always rides at the rear, as far away from him as he can get.

This portrait of a man who was responsible for the catering in one of the Inns of Court, the 'legal university' of the time, to which all barristers must still belong, seems rather slight. Its point is the cleverness of a servant by comparison with his employers, who are steeped in legal learning. Perhaps it has an artistic function too, in that it provides a sense almost of a physical barrier between the Miller and the Reeve, both unpleasant characters and strongly disliking one another. He tells an old and mildly scandalous tale of how the crow got its black feathers.

A gentil MAUNCIPLE was ther of a temple,	Maunciple.
Of which achatours mighte take exemple	
For to be wyse in bying of vitaille.	
For whether that he payde, or took by taille,	570
Algate he wayted so in his achat,	
That he was ay biforn and in good stat.	
Now is nat that of God a ful fair grace,	
That swich a lewed mannes wit shal pace	
The wisdom of an heep of lerned men?	575
Of maistres hadde he mo than thryes ten,	

567   *A gentil Maunciple was ther of a temple*: 'gentil' is used, as often, with a touch of irony. The man's job is menial: he looks after the catering at one of the four Inns of Court, as they are now known, to which all aspiring barristers must belong. Two, the Inner and Middle Temple, are so named – hence 'temple' here – because the Knights Templar had a house there until their order was dissolved nearly thirty years before Chaucer was born.

568   *achatours*: 'buyers' literally (cf. *acheter* in French), but by extension one who buys and provides for a household.

570–72   *For whether that ... good stat*: he studied the market so that he was always in credit – or, perhaps, so that he made a profit for himself, in view of later suggestions. To buy 'by taille' means to buy on credit, from the tally-sticks which were notched to record the amount, then split between buyer and seller so that neither could cheat the other when settling up. The usage survives oddly in the language of cricket, where runs were so recorded, and every twentieth run – to make adding-up easier – was cut or scored more deeply: hence to 'keep the score'.

573   *grace*: in the theological sense, an act or sign of God's mercy.

574   *pace*: 'outpace', 'outstrip'. There is a mildly cynical contrast between native shrewdness in an uneducated – 'lewed' – man and the ignorance in practical affairs of a whole 'heep' of men versed in legal niceties.

That were of lawe expert and curious;
Of which ther were a doseyn in that hous,
Worthy to been stiwardes of rente and lond
Of any lord that is in Engelond,   580
To make him live by his propre good,
In honour dettelees, but he were wood,
Or live as scarsly as him list desire;
And able for to helpen al a shire
In any cas that mighte falle or happe;   585
And yit this maunciple sette hir aller cappe.

577   *curious*: 'taking care', 'meticulous'.

579–83   *Worthy to been ... desire*: these lines indicate one of the occupations open to a man with some legal training. He could take care of the income and estates of a great noble, and, if he was honest and good at his job, could see to it that his employer always lived honourably free from debt on his own resources – or however economically he chose. Since nobles were rarely numerate, and it was considered beneath their rank to bother about money, they needed a shrewd and honest man to look after such things for them.

584–5   *And able for to helpen ... happe*: 'cas' can just mean any chance event, but it can also mean, as it still does, a law-suit or 'case', and that is perhaps what is here intended. If his employer became involved in a legal wrangle, his legally trained steward could help him out, or help him to help the district ('shire') if it were some major dispute over land.

586   *sette hir aller cappe*: a very colloquial phrase – 'Made fools of all of them'. This has led to widely varying interpretations of the Manciple's character: one is the picture of a rather sharp dealer, a lot cleverer than his learned masters in everyday business; another is a portrait of a swindler, who makes a lot of money for himself out of his supposed masters by buying cheap and cooking the accounts. Some remarks made to him by the Host later in *The Tales* suggest that the latter view may be correct.

The Reeve appears to be disliked by everyone. He rides alone at the rear of the company, as far away as he can get from the Miller, with whom he is on bad terms. His story, when he comes to tell it, is a very funny bedroom farce about a pretentious miller, drunken and dishonest. As the Miller is short, sturdy and noisy, the Reeve is lean and withdrawn. His job would make him unpopular, too: he acts as a sort of bailiff to a large estate, is a ruthless demander of rents, cannot be cheated but is dishonest himself. His rusty sword suggests he is no man of valour despite his choleric temperament – only he and the sanguine Franklin have their 'complexion' named. Perhaps the most important statement about him is that men feared him as they feared the Death (l. 605) – possibly the Black Death, the plague. This was always lying in wait, every summer, and no one knew where or whom it would strike. The portrait has, in fact, rather more sinister overtones than most.

The REVE was a sclendre colerik man,	Reve.
His berd was shave as ny as ever he can.	
His heer was by his eres round y-shorn.	
His top was dokked lyk a preest biforn.	590
Ful longe were his legges, and ful lene,	
Y-lyk a staf, ther was no calf y-sene.	
Wel coude he kepe a gerner and a binne;	
Ther was noon auditour coude on him winne.	
Wel wiste he, by the droghte, and by the reyn,	595
The yelding of his seed, and of his greyn.	
His lordes sheep, his neet, his dayerye,	
His swyn, his hors, his stoor, and his pultrye,	
Was hoolly in this reves governing,	
And by his covenaunt yaf the rekening,	600
Sin that his lord was twenty yeer of age;	
Ther coude no man bringe him in arrerage.	
Ther nas baillif, ne herde, ne other hyne,	
That he ne knew his sleighte and his covyne;	

588   *as ever he can*: medieval razors were not very efficient, but he has had as close a shave as was possible.

590   *lyk a preest*: the front part of his hair has been shaved as if he wore a priest's tonsure. This completes the initial picture of a mean man – hair, beard, even the top of his head, all close-cut. It is also a mark of servile status.

593   *Wel coude he kepe a gerner and a binne*: he knew how to look after a granary or a corn-bin, practical knowledge which would help him in his job as overseer of farm incomes on an estate.

594   *auditour*: perhaps here used rather in the sense of someone rendering an account rather than a man certifying that an account is correct.

596   *The yelding of his seed, and of his greyn*: some confusing grammar here. The 'his' probably refers to the farmer rendering an account rather than to the Reeve, who knew, from the weather, just what sort of crop to expect, and so could not be cheated by tales of a poor harvest.

597–8   *His lordes sheep … pultrye*: a battery of technical terms from farming. A simplified version would run: sheep, cattle bred for stock, milking-cows, pigs, horses, livestock generally and poultry.

600–601   *And by his covenaunt … age*: the Reeve was fortunate in having secured a contract, from the time his lord came of age, to be responsible for rendering an account of everything on the estate.

603   *Ther nas baillif, ne herde, ne other hyne*: 'baillif' is a problem, since in a sense that is what the Reeve was. It seems that he worked for a man of very large estates, who might have had several under-bailiffs, all answerable to the Reeve. A 'herde' was a herdsman or shepherd, 'hyne' meant a general farm labourer.

604   *That he ne knew his sleighte and covyne*: but the Reeve knew his tricks and deceptions. The double implication is that the Reeve was well versed in all the business of running an estate, and knew every man's job and the sort of crooked practice that might go with it; and that, as emerges later in the portrait, he was himself a man of crafty dishonesty, and so expert at detecting it in others.

They were adrad of him, as of the deeth. 605
His woning was ful fair up-on an heeth,
With grene treës shadwed was his place.
He coude bettre than his lord purchace.
Ful riche he was astored prively,
His lord wel coude he plesen subtilly, 610
To yeve and lene him of his owne good,
And have a thank, and yet a cote and hood.
In youthe he lerned hadde a good mister;
He was a wel good wrighte, a carpenter.

605 *They were adrad of him, as of the deeth*: it is not surprising that they all feared him as they did the plague itself. The portrait which has been built up to this line is of a mean creature, mean in appearance with his skinny legs and cropped hair, ruthless in exacting what was due and ready to spot any kind of fraud. At this point we might nevertheless think that that is what he is paid to do, and the picture is of a very competent, if hard, professional. The emphasis begins to shift on the very next line.

606 *His woning was ful fair up-on an heeth*: in praising his house, Chaucer suggests more than he says. Not many men in the Reeve's position could afford a fine house situated well away from the others – a situation which emphasizes his unsociable personality.

609–12 *Ful riche ... cote and hood*: these lines, which tell us how he afforded such a house, are not linguistically difficult, but the construction is not at first sight easy to unravel. The sense is that he knew various crafty ways of satisfying his noble employer by giving him or lending him from 'his owne' property. This is ambiguous, but 'his' implies that it was really his lord's property that the Reeve had filched or saved up, and was now handsomely lending back to its rightful owner, for which he was thanked, and was given a uniform as well.

613 *mister*: a 'trade'. We still speak of 'trade secrets', a survival of the word 'mystery' used to describe guilds and their crafts.

614 *wrighte*: an old irregular derivative, like 'wrought', of 'work', which survives in 'shipwright', 'cartwright', 'wheelwright' and, of course, in surnames. That he was a carpenter is an example of early plotting: Chaucer intended the Miller to tell a story about a skinny old carpenter.

This reve sat up-on a ful good stot,   615
That was al pomely grey, and highte Scot.
A long surcote of pers up-on he hade,
And by his syde he bar a rusty blade.
Of Northfolk was this reve, of which I telle,
Bisyde a toun men clepen Baldeswelle.   620
Tukked he was, as is a frere, aboute,
And ever he rood the hindreste of our route.

615   *stot*: what horsy people would now call a 'cob'. This is a small horse, sturdy, good at carrying weight, not highly bred or elegant in any way, a very workaday animal. It would be the sort of beast the Reeve probably rode about the estates, and serviceable for the purpose, though it seems he could have afforded better if he chose.

616   *That was al pomely grey, and highte Scot*: 'pomely' is 'dappled'. The beast's name has engendered an astonishing amount of academic speculation. One early editor was happy to inform us that 'Scot' was still a popular name for a horse in Norfolk, thus showing Chaucer's fidelity to detail. It has also been urged that the name was usually given to the best horse in the stable, because he gave good value for money, and an old meaning of 'scot' is tax, or rent, surviving in the north as 'scot and lot'. Perhaps we might agree that it was a common name for a horse and rhymes conveniently with 'stot', and let the matter rest there.

617   *A long surcote of pers*: his long blue surcoat is presumably not made of the 'pers' we have met elsewhere (an expensive slate-coloured material worn by the Doctor), because such a coat would be costly and indicate rank, whereas the Reeve is servile (judging by his cropped hair) and mean, and so would keep his wealth hidden.

618   *a rusty blade*: his rusty sword suggests some show of rank but little valour – he is not a man of violence, like his enemy the Miller. That it hints at impotence seems a rather post-Freudian notion, but some critics so read it.

620   *Baldeswelle*: this may have special significance. It was then part of the estate of the Earl of Pembroke, and his property had suffered some serious mismanagement by trustees. The Welsh Pembroke property had been in the care of one of Chaucer's friends, so he had an interest in the case.

622   *And ever he rood the hindreste of our route*: he always rode at the rear, and the Miller rode at the front (see also note to l. 566).

Though Chaucer often satirizes his characters, only in the last two
pilgrims do we get the strong impression that he actively disliked them.
The Summoner is a revolting man both physically and in his conduct of
his job. There is much argument about his ailment – those who believe
venereal disease existed in England this early naturally point to syphilis
– but it could well be pustular acne or even very severe psoriasis, which
in those times was often taken to be léprosy. His diet would hardly help
his inflamed face, and would make him a highly perfumed companion.
His job was to summon people to the ecclesiastical courts, which dealt
with moral offences, such as adultery, and were presided over by a bishop
or archdeacon. He also acted as a semi-official informer. Such a post was
open to corruption, and he is a very corrupt example indeed, actually
accepting bribes and encouraging the very sins he was supposed to report
for examination. The comic additions to his appearance, the garland and
the cake, or flat loaf of bread, suggest that he is drunk. Garlands were
hung up as inn-signs. His tale is one of the very few that almost every
reader, however liberal, would find disgusting.

A SOMNOUR was ther with us in that place,	Somnour.
That hadde a fyr-reed cherubinnes face,	
For sawcefleem he was, with eyen narwe.	625
As hoot he was, and lecherous, as a sparwe;	
With scalled browes blake, and piled berd;	
Of his visage children were aferd.	
Ther nas quik-silver, litarge, ne brimstoon,	
Boras, ceruce, ne oille of tartre noon,	630
Ne oynement that wolde clense and byte,	
That him mighte helpen of his whelkes whyte,	
Nor of the knobbes sittinge on his chekes.	
Wel loved he garleek, oynons, and eek lekes,	
And for to drinken strong wyn, reed as blood.	635
Thanne wolde he speke, and crye as he were wood.	
And whan that he wel dronken hadde the wyn,	
Than wolde he speke no word but Latyn.	
A fewe termes hadde he, two or three,	
That he had lerned out of som decree;	640
No wonder is, he herde it al the day;	
And eek ye knowen wel, how that a jay	

624 *cherubinnes*: a cherubic face still means a bright and boyish one. Medieval paintings in churches used brilliant colours, and cherubim and seraphim were the higher orders of angels, and were painted bright red. However, this face is not ablaze with the reflected glory of God, but with a disease.

625 *For sawcefleem he was, with eyen narwe*: 'sawcefleem' means 'spotty', from a supposed excess of salt in the phlegmatic humour. The narrow eyes may indicate either slyness or inflamed lids.

626 *sparwe*: sparrows were proverbially lecherous. Observation suggests that the proverb, like many others, has some truth in it.

627 *With scalled browes blake, and piled berd*: he had black, scabby or scaly eyebrows and a sparse beard. The eyebrows tend to confirm a diagnosis of severe psoriasis, but chronic barber's itch might account for the beard as well.

629–31 *Ther nas quik-silver ... byte*: a formidable array of ferocious medicaments – preparations based on mercury, lead, sulphur, borax, white lead and cream of tartar – most of which are poisonous, some very dangerous, and all as likely to irritate as to cure severe inflammation. The verb 'byte' well describes the searing effect some of these would have.

634–5 *Wel loved he garleek ... reed as blood*: it is of interest that he liked strong, common foodstuffs, rather than delicacies, and the red wine of the day was coarse. He would have reeked enough to offend even medieval nostrils.

636–41 *Thanne wolde he speke ... al the day*: when drunk he spoke only Latin, though he had merely picked up a few odd phrases from the legal documents which he heard regularly in the ecclesiastical courts.

642 *a jay*: jays were kept as cage-birds and taught to talk – the budgerigars of the time.

Can clepen 'Watte,' as well as can the pope.
But who-so coude in other thing him grope,
Thanne hadde he spent al his philosophye;   645
Ay '*Questio quid iuris*' wolde he crye.
He was a gentil harlot and a kinde;
A bettre felawe sholde men noght finde.
He wolde suffre, for a quart of wyn,
A good felawe to have his concubyn   650
A twelf-month, and excuse him atte fulle:
Ful prively a finch eek coude he pulle.

643   *Can clepen 'Watte,' as well as can the pope*: 'can say "Walter" as well
as the Pope can'. 'Watte' was a diminutive of Walter, then a very
popular name: witness the numbers of Watts and Watsons in any
modern directory. The Pope, of course, was the epitome of wisdom on
earth. The Summoner rattles off his scraps of Latin, as we should say,
'like a parrot'. Summoners were often not clergymen themselves,
though they worked for the Church, so they would have no formal
training in Latin.

644   *him grope*: 'get to grips with him', 'sound him out'.

645   *philosophye*: in the usual sense then of 'learning', 'wisdom'.

646   *Ay* 'Questio quid iuris' *wolde he crye*: 'he would always say, "I ask
what is the law on that matter"'. He must have heard this question, in
Latin, very often in the courts – 'What is the legal position?'

647   *a gentil harlot*: a 'harlot' is a 'rogue', though it had already also
acquired the sense of 'prostitute'. Here 'gentil' is used with obvious
irony.

648   *felawe*: 'companion' – he was 'a good sort' as we say.

649–51   *He wolde suffre ... atte fulle*: for the bribe of a quart of wine –
a very modest one – he would permit anyone he found to his liking to
keep a mistress for a year, and not report it to the courts. The use of
'concubyn' may indicate that the 'felawe' was a priest, and thus indeed
someone of his own sort in a way. Though priests did not marry, they
often had a mistress: in *The Reeve's Tale*, the Miller is married to the
daughter of such a union.

652   *Ful prively a finch eek coude he pulle*: this has two possible meanings.
It could mean that he knew how to make money out of gullible people;
or, remembering the modern colloquialism about 'pulling the birds', it
could mean, as seems likely, that he knew how to keep a lady-friend
for himself on the sly. So he was guilty of an offence he should have
reported, and encouraged others to follow him if he were bribed.

And if he fond o-wher a good felawe,
He wolde techen him to have non awe,
In swich cas, of the erchedeknes curs,   655
But-if a mannes soule were in his purs;
For in his purs he sholde y-punisshed be.
'Purs is the erchedeknes helle,' seyde he.
But wel I woot he lyed right in dede;
Of cursing oghte ech gilty man him drede –   660
For curs wol slee, right as assoilling saveth –
And also war him of a *significavit*.
In daunger hadde he at his owne gyse
The yonge girles of the diocyse,
And knew hir counseil, and was al hir reed.   665
A gerland hadde he set up-on his heed,
As greet as it were for an ale-stake;
A bokeler hadde he maad him of cake.

653–7   *And if he fond ... y-punisshed be*: probably this is the most serious condemnation, since it undermines the whole authority of the court, and the morality, which he was paid to uphold. In sum, he encouraged men he liked not to be afraid of being excommunicated by the arch-deacon, unless he kept his soul in his purse, because that is where he would be punished (by paying a fine – never mind whether he were penitent or not). He even suggests that archdeacons thought the same way, that as far as they were concerned, sin was a matter of paying cash for pardon.

659–61   *But wel I woot ... assoilling saveth* –: Chaucer makes one of his rare comments. He points out that excommunication kills (the soul, by damning it for ever to hell) and absolution saves. The two ideas are essentially complementary: we should fear the one, sincerely seek the other.

662   *a* significavit: forty days after excommunication, if a man still refused to pay his tithes (the commonest reason for this ban), a writ could be issued which began with this word, seeking his imprisonment.

663–5   *In daunger ... al hir reed*: the Summoner had under his authority the young folk ('girles' was used for both sexes) of the parish, knew all their secrets and was their chief adviser. This is a deplorable situation, since the whole portrait is one of utter corruption, and we now learn he had the young under his influence. Knowing their secrets, he could probably use them as spies, exert blackmail and extort other favours, as he pleased.

666- 8   *A gerland ... maad him of a cake*: the final picture is a symbol of drunken gluttony making a shameless exhibition of itself.

The Pardoner, like his companion, is presented in a thoroughly unpleasant light. The gross abuse of the sale of pardons was one of the causes of the Reformation. Pardoners sold what purported to be papal documents which gave absolution for sins: the original idea was that by giving a sum of money to the Church, as well as undergoing the essential act of contrition in yourself, you could be free of minor trespasses. This led to serious abuses. Pardoners sold fake documents, with relics as a sideline (as this one does), and claimed that the purchase of their documents could free men from the greatest sins with no more trouble than the paying for them. The Pardoner gives a completely frank account of his swindles before he tells his own story, which turns out to be a perfect little sermon, a parable about greed of all things, told with great skill and economy. Commentators sometimes suggest that he is effeminate or homosexual. Chaucer merely tells us that, whether by chance of birth or some later accident, he was not fully a man: hence the unbroken voice and hairless face. He makes a good foil to his friend the Summoner. Chaucer seems to have kept his most detestable characters until last. There is, however, to be one more.

With him ther rood a gentil PARDONER	Pardoner.
Of Rouncival, his freend and his compeer,	670
That streight was comen fro the court of Rome.	
Ful loude he song, 'Com hider, love, to me.'	
This somnour bar to him a stif burdoun,	
Was never trompe of half so greet a soun.	
This pardoner hadde heer as yelow as wex,	675
But smothe it heng, as dooth a strike of flex;	
By ounces henge his lokkes that he hadde,	
And ther-with he his shuldres overspradde;	
But thinne it lay, by colpons oon and oon;	
But hood, for jolitee, ne wered he noon,	680
For it was trussed up in his walet.	
Him thoughte, he rood al of the newe jet;	
Dischevele, save his cappe, he rood al bare.	
Swiche glaringe eyen hadde he as an hare.	

670   *Of Rouncival, his freend and his compeer*: 'Rouncival' is named after
      modern Roncesvalles in Spain, a religious house which had a subsidiary
      convent in London near to Charing Cross. It had a troubled history,
      and was notorious for its abuse of the right to sell indulgences.
      'His compeer' means 'his equal': the two wretches are indeed well
      matched.

672   *'Com hider, love, to me'*: a pop song of the time – 'Come and join
      me, sweetie'.

673   *a stif burdoun*: 'a strong bass part', or 'refrain'.

675–9 *This pardoner hadde heer . . . oon and oon*: 'strike' is a word still used
      by spinners, but 'hank' is better known. The picture is of hair that is
      lank – though he is proud of it. It may also be rather scanty, since 'his
      lokkes that he hadde' could imply that he had not many, and he spread
      them out so carefully over his shoulders to make them look thicker than
      they were, as a balding man will comb his hair carefully over the bare
      skin.

      Chaucer's detailed description here may be compared with that of the
      hair of Absolon in *The Miller's Tale*: the biblical character after whom
      he was named was a familiar symbol of worldly vanity, since it was
      because of his inordinately long hair that he was taken and killed.
      So vanity – even an effeminate vanity – may be an attribute of the
      Pardoner.

680   *for jolitee*: 'for fun', but perhaps also to show off, since we read in
      1.682 that he thought he was riding in the latest fashion ('newe jet').
      As the hood was a universal medieval garment, simple and useful for
      protection from sun, wind or rain, it was uncommon to dispense with
      it entirely out of affectation. To go completely bare-headed would have
      been almost indecent, and we notice he retains a small skull-cap.

684   *Swiche glaringe eyen hadde he as an hare*: he had eyes which bulged
      like a hare's. This pop-eyed appearance does not add to his attractions,
      but may have a deeper significance. The hare or rabbit still appears on
      German Easter cards, and is, like the familiar eggs of an English Easter,
      a symbol of fertility – Easter falls at about the time of the very ancient
      fertility rituals to do with the spring. So the hare might be a symbol not,
      as we should think, of timidity, but of lust. There is something very
      odd about the Pardoner's sexuality, and even, some people might
      think, about his relationship with the Summoner.

A vernicle hadde he sowed on his cappe.   685
His walet lay biforn him in his lappe,
Bret-ful of pardoun come from Rome al hoot.
A voys he hadde as smal as hath a goot.
No berd hadde he, ne never sholde have,
As smothe it was as it were late y-shave;   690
I trowe he were a gelding or a mare.
But of his craft, fro Berwik into Ware,
Ne was ther swich another pardoner.
For in his male he hadde a pilwe-beer,

685   *vernicle*: St Veronica has given her name to a pass in bull-fighting and a once-popular holy image. As Christ carried the Cross to Calvary, she wiped the sweat from his face, and an impression of it was left on the handkerchief she used. The Pardoner has an image of the face of the Suffering Christ stitched to his cap, as did many who had been to Rome.

687   *Bret-ful of pardoun come from Rome al hoot*: this line sounds like sales-talk – his bag was stuffed with pardons, 'hot from Rome'. Possibly, like his relics, they are fraudulent.

691   *I trowe he were a gelding or a mare*: this line has caused much pointless speculation. Clearly, as he is beardless and of unbroken voice, he is sexually incomplete, and the line rather unkindly suggests that this might be an accident of birth – he might as well have been born a woman, a 'mare' – or some disaster later in life which had deprived him of his virility, as happens to a gelding.

692   *fro Berwik into Ware*: Ware was the first town of any significance on the northern route out of London, Berwick the last before the Scottish border.

694   *pilwe-beer*: 'pillow-case' – another metathesis in the last syllable of 'pillow'.

Which that, he seyde, was our lady veyl: 695
He seyde, he hadde a gobet of the seyl
That sëynt Peter hadde, whan that he wente
Up-on the see, til Jesu Crist him hente.
He hadde a croys of latoun, ful of stones,
And in a glas he hadde pigges bones.   700
But with thise relikes, whan that he fond
A povre person dwelling up-on lond,
Up-on a day he gat him more moneye
Than that the person gat in monthes tweye.
And thus, with feyned flaterye and japes,   705
He made the person and the peple his apes.
But trewely to tellen, atte laste,
He was in chirche a noble ecclesiaste.
Wel coude he rede a lessoun or a storie,
But alderbest he song an offertorie;   710
For wel he wiste, whan that song was songe,
He moste preche, and wel affyle his tonge,
To winne silver, as he ful wel coude;
Therefore he song so meriely and loude.

695–701 *Which that ... thise relikes*: clearly these relics are fakes – bits of the Virgin's veil, of the sail of Peter the fisherman which he used before Christ summoned him to be his follower, the cross of cheap, flash alloy that looked like gold, with its stones probably no more than coloured glass, and a container with a collection of animals' bones made so that they could be seen without being removed, in the style of a 'monstrance', a device still used for the showing of sacred relics in Roman Catholic churches. It is easy for us to laugh at the gullibility of an age which could venerate things so obviously false. However, it is salutary to study seriously the sort of promises implied in modern advertising, and see that these are still largely aimed at our belief in magical powers to be found in a cosmetic or washing powder or slimming aid.

702 *up-on lond*: 'in a remote country district'. Such parsons, unlike the one of this pilgrimage, were often poorly educated and thus easy victims.

706 *and the peple*: this probably implies the parson's congregation.

708–9 *He was in chirche ... a storie*: 'in church he was a splendid figure of a churchman'(1.708) – he must have held authority at least to preach. By 'storie' may be meant a reading from one of the lives of the saints, but it is tempting to think it means what we should call a parable, since that is precisely what he tells – very well, too – in his own tale.

710–13 *But alderbest ... he ful wel coude*: 'offertorie' was the offering referred to in the portrait of the Wife of Bath. They were not offering to the Pardoner, but to the Church. The point is that after that he had to preach and, as he says, file his tongue until it was sharp enough to do its job well, because on his preaching depended his success in selling pardons.

714 *meriely*: there is a sly hint in this word that he looked forward to making money. His treble voice would be suitable for Church music.

This passage is of interest because in it Chaucer defends candour and honesty in art.

Now have I told you shortly, in a clause,   715
Thestat, tharray, the nombre, and eek the cause
Why that assembled was this companye
In Southwerk, at this gentil hostelrye,
That highte the Tabard, faste by the Belle.
But now is tyme to yow for to telle   720
How that we baren us that ilke night,
Whan we were in that hostelrye alight.
And after wol I telle of our viage,
And al the remenaunt of our pilgrimage.
But first I pray yow, of your curteisye,   725
That ye narette it nat my vileinye,
Thogh that I pleynly speke in this matere,
To telle yow hir wordes and hir chere;
Ne thogh I speke hir wordes properly.
For this ye knowen al-so wel as I,   730
Who-so shal telle a tale after a man,
He moot reherce, as ny as ever he can,
Everich a word, if it be in his charge,
Al speke he never so rudeliche and large;
Or elles he moot telle his tale untrewe,   735
Or feyne thing, or finde wordes newe.

715 *in a clause*: a mere figure of speech – 'in a few words'.

719 *the Belle*: this is the only mention of the Bell, presumably another inn.

722 *alight*: literally 'alighted', in the sense that they had got off their horses with the intention of staying.

725–36 *But first I pray yow ... wordes newe*: a passage of some importance and difficulty. He asks us not to attribute it to his lack of breeding ('vileinye') that he speaks plainly and repeats their very own words ('hir wordes properly'). His justification is that he wishes to tell his tale truthfully, and not start inventing or altering: thus he may have to speak 'rudeliche and large'. The interpretation of these words is tricky. By speaking plainly, does he mean crudely? Are we to take the last phrase as meaning 'coarsely and broadly'? Remembering those tales in which very blunt language is used – what we now call 'four-letter' words, though in his spelling five seems nearer the mark – it is easy to suppose that this is what he is talking about. An alternative suggestion may be that he had very little idea of one sort of vocabulary being indecent, as we have: if he wished to refer to a natural function, he used the common word, instead of drawing on the vocabulary of medicine or the nursery or employing a euphemism as we may do in 'polite' company. In these matters, the 'rudeness' that he speaks of probably lies more in the subject itself than in the words used. So possibly he is asking to be excused for using very plain English, instead of the fanciful literary language which was already being developed by teachers of rhetoric, and of which he makes fun in *The Franklin's Tale*:

> For th'orisonte hath reft the sonne his light;
> This is as muche to seye as it was night.

He may nat spare, al-thogh he were his brother;
He moot as wel seye o word as another.
Crist spak him-self ful brode in holy writ,
And wel ye woot, no vileinye is it.   740
Eek Plato seith, who-so that can him rede,
The wordes mote be cosin to the dede.
Also I prey yow to foryeve it me,
Al have I nat set folk in hir degree
Here in this tale, as that they sholde stonde;   745
My wit is short, ye may wel understonde.

737   *He may nat spare, al-thogh he were his brother*: a confused order of
words. The sense is that someone who repeats a story must do so
faithfully and in the exact words in which he had it – even if he had it
from his own brother.

739   *Crist spak him-self ful brode in holy writ*: this line supports the 'plain-
speaking' interpretation. In the Gospels Christ spoke in simple and
straightforward language, and, says Chaucer, there is nothing 'low' in
that.

741–2   *Eek Plato seith . . . cosin to the dede*: Plato was accessible to most
readers only in Latin versions, Greek being little known in England
until the next century. Chaucer may be having a small private joke: he
could not read Greek himself, but he had translated the work of
Boethius from Latin, and Boethius quotes Plato as saying exactly this
– the word must be cousin to the deed, meaning that the language must
fit the action described.

744   *Al have I nat set folk in hir degree*: the importance of rank and
precedence has already been touched on. He is possibly apologizing
quite sincerely for any chance error of protocol.

746   *My wit is short, ye may wel understonde*: to apologize for not being
very bright is a common trick of speakers, however, and presumably
here not intended seriously. It was one of the stock devices of rhetoric
referred to a few lines earlier.

After the odious Summoner and Pardoner we have one more pilgrim. He is important, though he never tells a story. The Host is a hearty man, good at being sociable with all sorts of men as a part of his job; though he keeps an eye on his profits, he also has an excellent hostelry, and he provides a valuable artistic link between one tale and the next, offering comments that are often salty and shrewd about the stories and their tellers.

<blockquote>

Greet chere made our hoste us everichon,
And to the soper sette he us anon;
And served us with vitaille at the beste.
Strong was the wyn, and wel to drinke us leste.   750
A semely man our hoste was with-alle
For to han been a marshal in an halle;
A large man he was with eyen stepe,
A fairer burgeys is ther noon in Chepe:
Bold of his speche, and wys, and wel y-taught,   755
And of manhod him lakkede right naught.
Eek therto he was right a mery man,
And after soper pleyen he bigan,
And spak of mirthe amonges othere thinges,
Whan that we hadde maad our rekeninges;   760
And seyde thus: 'Now, lordinges, trewely,
Ye been to me right welcome hertely:
For by my trouthe, if that I shal nat lye,
I ne saugh this yeer so mery a companye
At ones in this herberwe as is now.   765
Fayn wolde I doon yow mirthe, wiste I how.
And of a mirthe I am right now bithoght,
To doon yow ese, and it shal coste noght.

Ye goon to Caunterbury; God yow spede,
The blisful martir quyte yow your mede.   770
And wel I woot, as ye goon by the weye,
Ye shapen yow to talen and to pleye;
For trewely, confort ne mirthe is noon
To ryde by the weye doumb as a stoon;
And therfore wol I maken yow disport,   775
As I seyde erst, and doon yow som confort.
And if yow lyketh alle, by oon assent,
Now for to stonden at my jugement,

</blockquote>

750   *us leste*: an impersonal – 'we were very ready to drink'.

751–2   *A semely man ... in an halle*: the Host, in effect the last character of the pilgrimage, is described as a 'proper man', unlike the Pardoner, the last of the 'original' pilgrims. A 'marshal' had the task of seating people correctly in order in the 'hall' of a castle, where meals were taken. This involved a knowledge of precedence and the ability to speak properly to every different kind of person, important attributes in a publican with such a mixed clientele.

754   *A fairer burgeys is ther noon in Chepe*: more of a compliment than it seems. Southwark was outside London, and was considered a rather raffish place. Chepe, whose name survives in Cheapside, was a prosperous, mercantile quarter of the City. He may have lived in the dubious area of Southwark, but he was equal to any wealthy respectable citizen of London.

755   *bold of his speche*: 'he spoke with confidence'.

760   *Whan that we hadde maad our rekeninges*: he makes sure of their money before suggesting the 'mirth' he proposes.

761   *lordinges*: 'gentlemen'. He continues for some lines in a tone of high compliment. It sounds as though he was used to saying such things to every large and promising group of wayfarers.

765   *herberwe*: very similar to the word the Sailor uses for harbourage; here it means 'resting-place'.

766–7   *mirthe*: two grammatical uses of one word – he would be glad to entertain them and he has just thought of something entertaining.

768   *it shal coste noght*: his own eye for money perhaps makes him aware that other people like a bargain, so he urges that this will be free. In fact that is not quite the case, as we shall see.

770   *quyte yow your mede*: 'give you your reward', implying 'what you deserve', which in some cases is not much, as some of them are rogues.

772   *Ye shapen yow*: 'you intend'.

773   *confort*: this word still had some of its ancient sense of 'strengthen' (compare with 'fortify'), so here perhaps there is an idea of encouragement as well as merely pleasure, which is covered by 'mirthe'.

777   *by oon assent*: 'unanimously' – he wants no later arguments.

And for to werken as I shal yow seye,
To-morwe, whan ye ryden by the weye,   780
Now, by my fader soule, that is deed,
But ye be merye, I wol yeve yow myn heed.
Hold up your hond, withouten more speche.'
   Our counseil was nat longe for to seche;
Us thoughte it was noght worth to make it wys,   785
And graunted him withouten more avys,
And bad him seye his verdit, as him leste.
   'Lordinges,' quod he, 'now herkneth for the beste;
But tak it not, I prey yow, in desdeyn;
This is the poynt, to speken short and pleyn,   790
That ech of yow, to shorte with your weye,
In this viage, shal telle tales tweye,
To Caunterbury-ward, I mene it so,
And hom-ward he shal tellen othere two,
Of aventures that whylom han bifalle.   795
And which of yow that bereth him best of alle,
That is to seyn, that telleth in this cas
Tales of best sentence and most solas,
Shal have a soper at our aller cost
Here in this place, sitting by this post,   800

781–2 *Now, by my fader soule ... myn heed*: a good example of the difficulty of translating oaths. To swear by the soul of his departed father was probably a strong oath; to promise them his head if he didn't make them enjoy themselves is meaningless, mere emphasis.

783 *Hold up your hond, withouten more speche*: this brisk command, at the end of a fast and forceful speech, exemplifies what was meant by 'bold of his speche'. The whole effect is hearty, with an underlying sense that he has done it before and developed a good line in effective patter.

784 *Our counseil was nat longe for to seche*: 'counseil' means 'opinion', so the line can be translated as 'We soon made up our minds'.

785 *Us thoughte it was noght worth to make it wys*: an idiomatic line – 'We thought it was not worth making a great fuss about it'.

790–94 *This is the poynt ... othere two*: the Host here unfolds the scheme which Chaucer never managed to complete. As is made clear, they were to tell two stories each on the way to Canterbury ('To Caunterbury-ward') and two on the way home. In round numbers he must have been thinking of a hundred and twenty tales. He wrote twenty-three, of which some are incomplete, and one of those is told by a traveller who joins them on the way, the Canon's Yeoman.

795 *aventures that whylom*: the first word corresponds fairly closely to its modern form, 'adventures', though with a stronger sense of an element of chance. 'Whylom' was itself a traditional opening for a story: 'Once upon a time'.

798 *Tales of best sentence and most solas*: the Clerk's speech is full of high sentence – that is, of moral or serious meaning; but not all the stories are likely to be serious, so 'solas', 'amusement', is also to be counted.

800 *sitting by this post*: a nice forceful touch which brings the scene and speech to life. We can almost see the Host hitting the pillar beside him as he speaks.

Whan that we come agayn fro Caunterbury.
And for to make yow the more mery,
I wol my-selven gladly with yow ryde,
Right at myn owne cost, and be your gyde.
And who-so wol my jugement withseye   805
Shal paye al that we spenden by the weye.
And if ye vouche-sauf that it be so,
Tel me anon, with-outen wordes mo,
And I wol erly shape me therfore.'
   This thing was graunted, and our othes swore   810
With ful glad herte, and preyden him also
That he wold vouche-sauf for to do so,
And that he wolde been our governour,
And of our tales juge and reportour,
And sette a soper at a certeyn prys;   815
And we wold reuled been at his devys,
In heigh and lowe; and thus, by oon assent,
We been acorded to his jugement.
And ther-up-on the wyn was fet anon;
We dronken, and to reste wente echon,   820
With-outen any lenger taryinge.
   A-morwe, whan that day bigan to springe,
Up roos our host, and was our aller cok,
And gadrede us togidre, alle in a flok,
And forth we riden, a litel more than pas,   825
Un-to the watering of seint Thomas.
And there our host bigan his hors areste,
And seyde: 'Lordinges, herkneth, if yow leste.
Ye woot your forward, and I it yow recorde.
If even-song and morwe-song acorde,   830

803–4 *I wol my-selven ... be your gyde*: another appeal to the purse. He will ride with them without charge. How far they would need a 'gyde' on this well-trodden route is not clear, but perhaps he implies he knows the best places to stay – in any case, it sounds impressive.

805–6 *And who-so ... by the weye*: while it is idle to speculate what *The Tales* would have been like if they had been completed, who would have won the supper and the rest of it, there seems here a strong hint that Chaucer intended some sort of dispute to arise on the journey so that the Host could invoke this rule, that anyone who disagreed with his judgement should pay all their expenses. The Host does, in fact, provide much more than a mere linking figure: some of his comments are pungent and funny, and he asserts his authority when it is necessary without hesitation.

812 *vouche-sauf*: that he would 'condescend'. His politeness is returned.

814–16 *And of our tales ... at his devys*: he is asked to judge the stories and act as foreman of the jury too – that is, 'report' his verdict on them. It is not clear where the idea of the feast in honour of the winner comes from; but as the Host always has an eye on profit, it seems likely that he suggested it. He thus ensures that a large group will return, pass at least a night with him and pay for an expensive meal – though they do fix the price in advance.

817 *In heigh and lowe*: 'in all affairs, great and small'.

823–4 *Up roos our host ... alle in a flok*: anyone who has seen a cockerel fussing his hens along will think that this line suggests much more than that the Host woke them up – he gets them moving too.

825 *a litel more than pas*: 'a little faster than a walking pace' – they jogged gently for the first couple of miles, which is good, practical horsemanship.

826 *watering of seint Thomas*: watering-places for horses and other animals were important points. This stream, on what was then called the Kent Road, was later considered a sufficiently public spot for Surrey executions to take place there, just as Tyburn (the Tye Burn, or brook) near modern Marble Arch did, to the north-west of London, on the opposite side.

830 *If even-song and morwe-song acorde*: 'If evensong and matins are in harmony' – that is, if you agree this morning with what you said last night.

Lat se now who shal telle the firste tale.
As ever mote I drinke wyn or ale,
Who-so be rebel to my jugement
Shal paye for al that by the weye is spent.
Now draweth cut, er that we ferrer twinne;   835
He which that hath the shortest shal biginne.
Sire knight,' quod he, 'my maister and my lord,
Now draweth cut, for that is myn acord.
Cometh neer,' quod he, 'my lady prioresse;
And ye, sir clerk, lat be your shamfastnesse,   840
Ne studieth noght; ley hond to, every man.'
    Anon to drawen every wight bigan,
And shortly for to tellen, as it was,
Were it by aventure, or sort, or cas,
The sothe is this, the cut fil to the knight,   845
Of which ful blythe and glad was every wight;
And telle he moste his tale, as was resoun,
By forward and by composicioun,
As ye han herd; what nedeth wordes mo?
And whan this gode man saugh it was so,   850
As he that wys was and obedient
To kepe his forward by his free assent,
He seyde: 'Sin I shal biginne the game,
What, welcome be the cut, a Goddes name!
Now lat us ryde, and herkneth what I seye.'   855
    And with that word we riden forth our weye;
And he bigan with right a mery chere
His tale anon, and seyde in this manere.

835   *draweth cut*: an imperative – 'draw lots'. He is using an old and simple method of picking someone, by holding out a fistful of straws, one of which has been cut short. Whoever draws it is the chosen person. This is still done – matches are often used – and those who have done it will know that there is a certain knack in presenting the handful of ends so that a predetermined person is often the one who, apparently by chance, draws the shortened stick or straw.

837–40   *Sire knight . . . lat be your shamfastnesse*: we now see the Host's skill in addressing everyone suitably, as a 'marshal in a hall' would have known how to do and every good publican still does. He addresses the highest of rank first, with great deference. The Prioress fancies herself as a lady and is a Church dignitary anyway, so she is first spoken to politely. The Clerk is poor, and gets a rough 'sir clerk' and an order to abandon his modest shyness. All imperatives are in the polite plural, except 'lat be' to the Clerk.

841   *Ne studieth noght*: possibly an order to the Clerk to stop thinking and get on with it. But 'study' is still used in northern speech in the sense of 'think over carefully', and he may be asking all of them not to ponder their choice, not to 'make it wys' in fact.

844   *Were it by aventure, or sort, or cas*: these words all imply different sorts of chance – 'by chance, fate or mere luck'. The unnecessary repetition suggests that the Host had arranged the draw so that the senior person present should lead off, an arrangement with which no one could quarrel, as, indeed, no one does.

851–4   *As he that wys . . . a Goddes name!*: we remember that the Knight was a courteous man, and he is 'wys' or prudent too, so he accepts the draw without demur or any false protestation and gets on with the story in his homely way at once. That he welcomes it 'a Goddes name' may be more than a mere oath. He is a devout man, and this is a sort of blessing on the little enterprise he is to lead.

Their horses being watered and the first teller chosen, they ride on, to listen to a lengthy tale of love and chivalry.

5. Further considerations

We began this short study of *The Prologue* by asking two questions. What did this mean when it was written? What does it mean now? Perhaps we have come nearer to an answer to the first of these, but we have surely realized that there can never be a satisfactory and complete answer to it, which does not mean that it is not an interesting and worthwhile subject to pursue. For many users of this book, a brief, wry answer to the second question might be: 'It means I have to pass an examination on the text.' It is a pity that Chaucer was unable to include a Gentil Examiner in his portrait gallery, but the species did not then exist.

Some guides to study include examples of typical examination questions, but we shall not do so here. Instead, we might briefly consider, or reconsider, some of the ideas that have been discussed in the course of these notes.

Perhaps the most obvious topic for us to look at again is Chaucer's view of and way of presenting *character*. Are we any nearer to an understanding of the three main sorts of characterization mentioned in Chapter 2? These were the pilgrims who are merely mentioned, those who appear to be types personifying some vice or virtue perhaps, and those three-dimensional figures which come alive as we read and appear to us as 'real'.

Now that we have worked our way through the text, we may see this question in a slightly different way, because we have looked at all the characters in the order in which Chaucer presents them, and can hardly suppose that it was a random one. We have noted, in passing, the importance of rank in the medieval world, and that Chaucer begins with men of high rank. He ends with a couple of downright rogues, and it is tempting to seek out some pattern to account for the position of everyone on the pilgrimage between the two. There are two cautions to bear in mind in any such scheme, however. We do not know the order in which the pilgrims rode, except that they were led by the Miller with his bagpipes, while the Reeve, who disliked him and almost everyone else apparently, brought up the rear. The Summoner and Pardoner rode side by side, singing their dubious repertoire of songs, and some of the pilgrims would obviously have been grouped because they were together in a special sense: the Knight, Squire and Yeoman; the Prioress and her sister-nuns and their priest; the Guildsmen of 'one fraternity' and so on. The other problem is that we have great difficulty in defining classes in a meaningful way, despite the popularity of sociology as a contemporary study, and often find ourselves betrayed into such expressions as 'middle middle class' and the like. We have a special problem with the word 'professional', which has changed its meaning quite a lot in the last fifty years – 'he takes a very professional attitude'; 'the best tennis-players usually go professional'; 'the learned professions'; 'he's a professional soldier'. These expressions give us some notion of how loosely the word can be used. To Chaucer himself the word meant what it still means in the Church – a 'profession' of faith. We would still call a doctor a professional man, and use the same expression of a lawyer; but the Clerk is not, in our sense, a professional scholar, nor the Knight a professional soldier.

It is therefore suggested that any elaborate scheme of precedence in the ordering of the characters, such as some editors offer their readers, should be treated with reservation, though these schemes are often well supported and are certainly of interest. We may find it easier to make some rather crude divisions, examine each one in the light of our previous study and consider whether we can draw any conclusions about Chaucer's attitudes to them and what they did or did not do in the world.

The most obvious divisions – though there is some overlap – seem to be: the aristocrats; the Church; the pilgrims who have some sort of skill or profession by which they live; the exceptionally humble; and, of course, the rogues, who appear in all but the first and last of these groups. We shall consider them in this order.

The aristocrats

These form a clearly defined group: the Knight, the Squire and their single attendant, who may be considered with them as a reflection of his employers, the Yeoman.

The *Knight*, as we have seen, is something of an idealized portrait, and unmistakably old-fashioned. He still goes to war in chain-mail, by then a form of armour that was out of date, and the campaigns he went on suggest something of the Crusader. He is reserved, but ready to play his part in the story-telling game, and in his story he shows not only a very strong sense of the realities of battle and of single combat, but also of the old code of chivalrous behaviour which bound even mortal enemies to respect one another. He also makes a few dry observations on the effect of love, which perhaps spring from his observation of his own son.

The *Squire* is indeed a lover – at his age we should expect it – and he appears at first to be the very opposite of his father, dressed in the latest fashion and with all sorts of accomplishments that have nothing to do with the art of war: literacy, music, drawing and so on. Yet he too has been a warrior from an early age, and has done well in the field for one so young. The portraits surely complement one another – the old world and the new in two generations.

The picture is rounded off by the *Yeoman*. He is no aristocrat – he does not pretend to be one, with his cropped hair – but he is a man of obvious efficiency, dressed in the colour of his work as a forester, very well equipped with appropriate weapons, protected by the badge of his patron saint, his sole concession to ornament being the handsome bracer – perhaps of tooled leather – that was a part of his working gear. He is not unlike the description of the Knight's horses – good, but not of a showy nature.

There seems no doubt that Chaucer presents these three with respect for all of them: the Knight possesses old-fashioned virtues, piety, courteous speech and integrity; his son belongs to a different world, with more fashionable accomplishments, but these obviously make him more attractive, and he has the basic virtues of courage and fidelity to his father as well; the Yeoman is businesslike, a quality Chaucer would have had occasion to respect in the various offices he held himself. The overall picture of the aristocracy seems to be that it is changing, but not in the things that really matter.

The Church

This is a much more difficult group to deal with, as so many people of the period were in some way connected with the Church, and not all of them were in Holy Orders or members of a monastic or similar institution. In a sense the Clerk is a Churchman, the Summoner works for the Church, the Pardoner makes a living out of it and even the Guildsmen may have belonged to an organization that had its origin in a parochial or charitable foundation. The simplest approach is to look at the pilgrims who have any ecclesiastical connection in the order in which they appear in *The Prologue*.

The *Prioress* is the first to appear, immediately after the aristocrats, to whose society she has some pretensions to belong: she takes pains to assume courtly manners, we are told. She is essentially a vain woman, more concerned with social standing than with charity, with dressing to the best advantage rather than with her vow of poverty. The best we can say of her is that she is harmless, and Chaucer seems, on the whole, to find her rather amusing. Her retinue remains anonymous, though her priest tells a funny, if rather literary, story.

The *Monk*, on the other hand, is more difficult to assess. He follows the Prioress aptly enough, since he is a man of some standing in the monastic world, with the right to leave his monastery and oversee outlying property. He is greedy, possibly a womanizer, certainly a man of wealth with his costly hunters and expensive harness; but above all he not only flagrantly breaks the monastic rules, but publicly abuses them as out-dated. Though Chaucer tells us that he agreed with him, it is hard to think that he did so out of more than politeness. The man abuses the very system which gives him such a self-indulgent life, and this is never an attractive trait. As for 'poring upon a book', Chaucer certainly respected the learning which the monasteries still promoted: the question 'How shall the world be served?' is surely loaded – the Monk should not be serving the world at all, but God. As for the austere life of labour and piety, some half-dozen Carthusian monasteries were set up in England during Chaucer's life, and this order has retained to the present day its absolute adherence to the old principles of the contemplative life. Chaucer may not have thought this the best way to live, but he surely does not approve of a man who so blatantly has his swan and eats it.

The *Friar* is easier to grasp. He is an out-and-out rogue, who abuses his position to his own profit and who frankly undermines the teaching of the Church. Here Chaucer emphasizes the Friar's refusal to have anything to do with those with whom he should be most concerned – the sick and needy.

At this point Chaucer moves away from the Church, though the Clerk is the next character but one to be introduced, and he would be in Minor Orders. He takes up the theme much later in the Parson, and to some extent in his lay equivalent, his brother the Ploughman.

The *Parson* is easily dismissed as an idealized character, too good to be true. Experience suggests that this is not so: there *are* saints in this world, though they take some finding. What Chaucer has clearly done is to take the teaching of Christ to his followers very seriously, and point out that this was how he ordered all who followed him to behave, even down to the staff which the Parson carries as he walks the length and breadth of his scattered parish. The Parson never abuses his power or learning (we note this humble man is a graduate) and he is more ready to forgive than to condemn. In his own sphere of life he is a pattern of Christianity, as the Knight is in his, and as the Ploughman is at the other end of the social scale.

The *Ploughman* is a practical lay Christian, always ready to do his duty by the Church – he pays his tithes promptly – but also by his fellow, helping out where help is needed, and asking no reward.

From this devout, unostentatious couple, who are the sole representatives of the 'very humble' group, there is a further jump to the end of the list, where we meet two unequivocal rogues.

The *Summoner* shares the basic fault of the Monk and Friar: he abuses his position and encourages a wrong attitude to the Church he supposedly serves. He is also a good example, like the Miller, of someone to whom our attitude is largely based on physical appearance, besides direct comment. The first things we are told about him are the disgusting details of his facial affliction, and that he was as sexy as a sparrow. He is also a drunkard and a moral pervert. He brings the Church and its teachings into utter disrepute, encouraging the very sins he should report, deriding excommunication, accepting bribes, using young folk as spies. There seems every indication that Chaucer despised and detested such men.

The *Pardoner*, as he is described, is apparently his 'compeer' in every respect – some commentators even think that a homosexual alliance is hinted at. What certainly binds them together is greed, the *cupiditas* of the Latin Bible, inadequately translated as 'love of money' for it embraces every kind of greediness and grabbing. He too betrays the Church he serves. His phoney relics devalue the ones Chaucer believed to be genuine; he battens upon the poor, just as the Friar is parasitic upon the rich; he keeps back most of what he gets instead of giving it to the Order to which it should go; he is vain of his appearance, like the Prioress but with much less reason; he is impotent (the subject of a harsh joke from the Host later in *The Tales*); and his one talent, that of preaching well, is put to an ill use, gain. He tells a perfect little parable when it is his turn to speak, and at once follows it up with a blatant piece of sales-talk patter, urging them all to roll up and buy his wares. The abuse of the sale of indulgences was by this time a notorious scandal, and Chaucer is reflecting only what a lot of good churchmen would have thought; but the portrait is tinged with something as near to malice as anything we can find in his writing. There is no kindliness here, no saving grace to be found.

Chaucer's view of the Church, then, could be stated simplistically: he approved of what was good in it, but was aware of and critical of what was bad. This does not get us very far. Perhaps the key lies in the sin which he shows as common to all those he condemns most clearly – the sin of betraying your own faith, whether with glib excuses like the pleasure-loving, world-serving Monk, or outrageously like the Summoner encouraging the vices he should condemn and the Friar mocking poverty, or hypocritically like the Pardoner pretending men are in serious need of salvation so that he can sell them the means. The minor abuses of the comfortable clerics, such as the Prioress and the Monk, are noted more with irony than with condemnation. His whole-hearted admiration is for those who set a Christian example in a simple and charitable life.

The professionals

Our third group of pilgrims, those who live by some sort of skill or profession, begins with the Merchant, with whom it is convenient to group the Doctor and Lawyer as men whom we should still call professionals.

The *Merchant* would today be a financier, perhaps. He is a skilful businessman, clever in maintaining what we should call his 'image' of prosperity even when he is in debt, talking incessantly of his profits, manipulating exchange rates to his advantage. The portrait is oddly noncommittal, perhaps of a class rather than of a person, though some editors think his headgear might have identified him to the original hearers.

The *Serjeant of Law* is more complex. Few men love a lawyer. Chaucer appears to praise him for his 'wise words' and his discreet air, as well as his encyclopedic knowledge of cases and judgements. Yet there is a double edge to the commendation. His particular skill in the handling of land deals suggests that he is capable of shady practice, and the whole portrait reminds us again and again that he worked for money. The law should not, in the end, be something that is bought and sold.

The *Doctor* is similarly ambiguous. He too is learned – in fact his learning, both in astronomy and in authors ancient and modern, is so lengthily emphasized that we wonder if it is not deliberately overdone in order to suggest the theoretical rather than the practical man of medicine. His temperate habits and sober dress, befitting his station and profession, are apparently noted with approval; yet he works hand in glove with the pharmacist, each making money for the other, and his love of gold – which he made in quantity when the plague was severe – is the final touch of the portrait. Perhaps we are to think that he, like the Lawyer, makes his money out of the distress of others.

We are now left to consider others who had lesser skills, and a few who do not readily fit into this or any other sort of classification.

The *Clerk* is a man of learning, though he does not teach in a professional sense: he does it as 'gladly' as he learns, so presumably it is free. He is the very opposite of many of the characters we have been looking at, for he has no money or interest in making it. Whatever he comes by goes on the means to study. The portrait is affectionate, slightly amusing, that of an utterly unworldly scholar in a pageant of worldly people. There is an implied contrast between him and the immediately preceding pilgrim, the Merchant: the latter's speech is always about profit, the former's about morality.

The *Guildsmen* may be linked with the Prioress and perhaps the Franklin, as we have seen, since they have social pretensions. This is manifested in their silver-mounted knives (illegal, unless they had property worth £500, which would be most unlikely) and their general self-importance, more appropriate to members of one of the great city guilds than to these big fish in a tiny puddle. There is an oblique glance at the pressure put upon them by their wives to seek the highest civic status. As they made a good income, they were presumably good at their jobs.

The *Cook* is good at his, and we are given details of his skills. The portrait is achieved almost wholly in this way, but has just two touches, both somewhat unpleasant, of direct description: he is a big drinker; and he has some sort of open ulcer on his leg, a repulsive detail, even in less squeamish times, in a man whose business was the preparation of food. Chaucer, unusually for him, makes a direct comment on it.

The *Shipman* appears next, and again there is a list of his skills. Chaucer must have dealt with many such men in the Port of London, for he obviously knows a lot about the perils of navigation, and some of the tricks of the trade too, such as how to filch wine from the cargo and the quickest way with pirates. Perhaps the key to this picture is its strangeness. Sailors were a breed apart. As such men go, he was a good, if not very scrupulous man, and we may feel a tinge of amusement at him in his unfamiliar situation – riding awkwardly on his wretched nag, and his dress, and presumably his West Country speech and weather-beaten colouring marking him out from his fellows.

The *Wife of Bath* has a skill too, and a good one in which she is very proficient, though we tend to remember her for her secondary accomplishments. The portrait is a full and rich one, with a variety of devices used to enliven it: her trade, her dress, even her spurs, her colouring, her teeth, her numerous journeyings and numerous husbands, her easy-going social manner and her independence of character. This was attributable to her two skills: as a good weaver, she could earn well; and as an avowed man-hunter she had secured – as we later learn – a lot of money from the elderly men she had married and exhausted by her demands. The portrait, which is greatly amplified when she comes to tell her own story, is full of vitality. Chaucer seems to have enjoyed creating her, if indeed she is not drawn from real life.

The *Miller* is robustly presented too, and a man of some prosperity, but the resemblance ends there. He is described almost like an animal, and much animal imagery is used in the portrait. A hefty brute of a man, perhaps, because he is so strong, more than a little dangerous when he is drunk, and, as all millers were said to be, a thief, he is nevertheless a great teller of coarse stories. So was Chaucer, but Chaucer always told a story well, whatever its subject-matter. The Miller is all mouth.

The *Manciple* is a man of minor skill – he caters for a college or hall of law students, and we are told nothing of his appearance, simply that he was good at a bargain. There is an implied distinction between his native cunning and the inability of his learned employers to cope with the real world of buying and selling. How to evaluate this we do not know. The carpenter in *The Miller's Tale* is the embodiment of this view, and he is made an utter fool of in the end by a student.

The *Reeve* is the last in this group, as he rides last in the cortège, and he is one of the more fully drawn characters. Appearance, dress, weaponry, horse, home, all are accounted for; but above all it is emphasized how well he knew his job, so much so that everyone feared him. The total impression is of a mean man, a solitary, quick to deal with any default and skilful at lining his own pockets. He rides alone, and we can see why.

Is it possible to come to any conclusions from this very mixed group? Chaucer seems to have respected anyone who was good at his job, but had some reservations when considering the jobs themselves. Thus the Doctor and Lawyer are not wholly comfortable portraits, since these men live on the misfortunes of their fellows. The Reeve and Miller do useful jobs, but the former probably and the latter certainly exploit their position for their own gain. So, arguably, does the Manciple. The Shipman lives a dangerous life and is allowed his occasional lack of scruple. The Guildsmen are harmlessly amusing.

We have not succeeded in isolating a separate group of rogues, but we are now in a position to try to establish how Chaucer thought about roguery. In this he seems to take the view that most of us would share. An amusing rogue is forgiven much by those who know him, so the Miller is let off lightly in this respect and the Wife of Bath, loud and promiscuous as she is, is likeable enough. The rogue that Chaucer dislikes is the man who has a serious influence in the world and misuses it profoundly: so the Friar, Summoner and Pardoner are dealt with much more severely than the indulgent Monk. Yet Chaucer is rare to condemn, or to give a wholly one-sided picture. Like most great authors, he understands well enough that we are not black or white, but mostly different shades of grey.

Grey the pictures themselves never are. He has many ways of making his impression on the reader: by describing table-manners, as with the Prioress; by their speech, as in her case, or in that of the Clerk and the Host; by their horses and horsemanship – the Shipman on his nag, the Ploughman on his humble mare, the Knight with excellent but un-ostentatious mounts, the Wife of Bath with spurs as sharp as her tongue; most notably by items of dress, from the quietly expensive robe of the Doctor to the Squire's fashionable display, the Knight's stained tunic, the Pardoner's attempts to be in the latest style. There is, too, a host of apparently random items – the Monk's favourite dish, the name of the Reeve's horse, the carefully anonymous Merchant. What are we to make of these?

Scholars – and by trying, however modestly, to understand Chaucer a little for ourselves, we have entered their ranks – have spent lifetimes in considering such problems. Chaucer, no mean scholar himself, knew how to sum up the hopelessness of mortal endeavour – 'The lyf so short, the craft so long to lerne' – but even here, true to his medieval self, he is quoting earlier authority: he is translating an author the Doctor had read, Hippocrates, who had said this of his own 'craft' of medicine about eighteen hundred years earlier. We are still learning.

Bibliography

There is a wealth of books about Chaucer, most of them too specialized and nearly all of them too expensive for the average student's needs or means. The simplest criterion is to find what is available from libraries.

Complete Texts of *The Canterbury Tales*

The most authoritative edition is *The Complete Works of Geoffrey Chaucer*, edited by F. N. Robinson, Oxford University Press, 1951. This is a substantial work, but good libraries should have it. Less elaborate, but very respectable, is the complete *Chaucer* of W. W. Skeat in the Oxford Standard Authors series, Oxford University Press, 1973. A modestly priced edition of *The Canterbury Tales* only, with marginal notes on difficult words, is produced in the Everyman series by Dent, 1981.

The Prologue

There are many editions of this, most of them published for use in schools, but a few aiming at a rather higher academic level. The present writer has found the edition by Phyllis Hodgson, published by the University of London Athlone Press, 1969, to be the most stimulating and provocative.

Modern Versions

The most popular remains the 'translation' into modern verse made by Nevill Coghill, published by Penguin (1951). It is lively reading, though there is a good deal of padding and modifying in order to maintain a rhyme scheme. For a straightforward prose version, which tries to keep close to the original but retains some of its vitality, you might find that by Stephen Coote in the Passnotes series, *Chaucer: The General Prologue to The Canterbury Tales*, Penguin Books, 1985, to be a useful standby. Though the book is aimed at a slightly different target, it contains much interesting and useful information.

Background

Still available in libraries is the excellent *Chaucer* by M. W. Grose, published by Evans Brothers, 1967 – short, but full of information clearly presented. The appropriate volume of the Pelican Guide to English Literature, *The Age of Chaucer*, edited by Boris Ford, Penguin Books, 1954, is an obvious choice.

More specialized treatment of topics we have touched on is to be found in Ian Robinson's *Chaucer's Prosody*, Cambridge University Press, 1971, which deals at length with the problems of the verse structure; and language is examined very thoroughly in R. M. V. Elliot's *Chaucer's English*, André Deutsch, 1974. Both are substantial volumes, but a good library should have them.

a in
a-morwe on the following morning
a-sonder apart
absolucion absolution
achat purchase
achatours purchasers; caterers
acordaunt agreeable to
acorde agree
acorded suitable
adrad afraid
adversitee adversity
aferd afraid
affyle make smooth
after according to
after oon one invariable
   standard
ageyn against
alderbest best of all
alderman municipal or guild officer
ale-stake a garland in front of an
   ale house
algate always
Algezir Algeciras
Alisaundre Alexandria
aller everybody's
alwey always
alyght alighted; staying
amblere an easy-to-ride, ambling
   horse
amiable friendly
anlas a short two-edged knife or
   dagger
anon soon
apes dupes
apothecaries apothecaries,
   pharmacists

apyked trimmed
aqueyntaunce, have associate with
areste bring to a halt
aright certainly
array dress, clothing
arrerage arrears
Artoys Artois
arwes arrows
aryve disembarkation (of troops)
as nouthe as of now, just now
ascendent asscendant (an
   astrological term)
assent agreement, accord
assente agree
assoilling absolution
assyse assizes
astored provided
astronomye astronomy
atones at once, at one time
auditour accountant
aught all
Austin Augustine
avaunce profit
avaunt boast
aventure accident
avys discussion
ay always

baar carried
bacheler aspirant after knighthood
baggepype bagpipes
baillif superintendent, bailiff
bake baked
balled bald
bar carried
baren conducted

barres bands

batailles combats

bawdrik a belt worn across the
chest and under the arm, a sling

bedes beads, a rosary

beggestere beggar woman

Belmarye a heathen kingdom,
Morocco

ben be

benefice, benefyce job as parish
priest or other religious office

Beneit Benedict

benigne kindly

berd beard

berye berry

bever beaver fur

bifel befell, happened

biforn before; in credit

binne bin for storing grain

bisette employed

bisier busier

bisinesse work

bismotered dirtied

bisyde near; the suburbs of

bit bade

blankmanger white meat with rice,
milk, sugar and almonds

bledde bleeding

blew blue

blisful blessedly happy

blythe happy

bokeler, bokelor small shield

Boloigne Boulogne

bootes boots

boras borax

bord dais, table of state

born conducted

bote remedy

botes boots

bracer protection for the arm
against bowstrings

braun muscle

breed bread

breem bream

breke break

bret-ful brimful

bretherhed brotherhood, fraternity

brimstoon sulphur

Britayne Brittany

brode broadly; in an uneducated
way

broille broil

brooch broach

brood broad

brustles bristles

brydel bridle

brynge call

Burdeux-ward from Bordeaux

burdoun refrain; accompaniment

burgeys prosperous citizen

but-if unless

by-cause since

byng buying

byte cauterize

caas case

calf calf, lower part of leg

can knows about

cappe, sette hir aller beat them all

carf carve

carie lift

carl fellow

carpe chat animatedly

Cartage Carthage; Cartagena in
Spain

cas chance, instance

catel possessions, property

caughte took

ceint girdle

celle small monastery

certen agreed, fixed; certainly

ceruce salve made of white lead

chambres rooms

chaped capped

chapman merchant

charitee charity

chaunterie endowed chapel where founder's soul is prayed for

chekes cheeks

Chepe Cheapside

chere behaviour; entertainment

cherubinnes like a cherub or angel

chevisaunce borrowing money on credit

chiknes chickens

chirche church

chivachye (cavalry) expeditions

chyn chin

clause few words

clennesse cleanliness

clense cleanse

cleped called, named

clerk postgraduate scholar

cloysterer monk in monastery

cofre coffer

cok cockerel

colerik quick-tempered

Coloigne Cologne

colpons portions

compaignye company; close friends; lovers

complexioun humour, temperament

composicioun agreement

concubyn mistress

condicioun nature, inner and outer

contree country; part of country, district

coold cold

cop top

cope priest's cloak

coppe cup, beaker

corage heart

cordial something that stimulates the heart

cosin resemble; be at one with

cote coat, outer garment

coude know how to, knew how to

counseil opinion

countour auditor of accounts

countrefete imitate

cours course; journey

couthe known of, knew how to

couthe, as he as best he could

covenaunt agreement

coverchiefs kerchiefs, headscarves

covyne deceitful agreement

coy shy

Cristen Christian

Cristendom Christian countries

Cristofre a medallion of St Christopher

croppes tips, shoots

crowned with a crown on top

croys cross

crulle curled

cryke creek

curat parish priest

cure care

curious elaborate, meticulous

curs curse

cursen excommunicate

cursing cursing

curteisye courtesy, etiquette

curteys courteous

cut lots (as in 'draw lots')

daliaunce gossip

daunger within his jurisdiction; danger, risks

daungerous difficult to approach

dayerye dairy

dayesye daisy

deed dead
deef deaf
deeth death, the plague
degree social status
del time
deliver nimble, agile
delve dig
delyt pleasure
depe deeply
Dertemouthe Dartmouth
desdeyn badly
despitous full of contempt
dettelees in credit
devys direction
devyse tell of
deyntee thoroughbred (of a horse)
deyntees dainties
deys dais, raised platform
diete diet
digestible easily digested
digne worthy; superior
diligent attentive
diocyse diocese
dischevele with hair hanging loose
discreet tactful
dispence expenditure
disport geniality; recreation, diversion
divyne divine
dokked tonsured, cropped
domes judgements
dong dung
doon do; go on
dooth does
dore door
dormant permanent
dorste dared, dare
doseyn dozen
doumb dumb
draughte drink
dresse arrange; prepare; look after

drogges drugs
droghte drought, dryness
drye dry
dwellynge living
dyere a dyer of cloth
dyke make ditches

ecclesiaste churchman
eek also
elles, ellis else
embrouded embroidered
encombred stuck
endyte compose, draw up, write
engendred engendered, produced, begotten
enoynt anointed
ensample example
entuned intoned
envyned stored with wine
Epicurus Epicurus (philosopher of pleasure)
erchedeknes archdeacon's
erst before; just now
erys ears
eschaunge money-markets
esed accommodated; entertained
estat fettle; condition; social status
estatlich, estatly stately
esy easy, undemanding, moderate
even-song evensong
evene ordinary; moderate
everich each, every
everichon everyone
evermore always
every-deel all of them
exemple example
eyen eyes

facultee ability
fader father
fair language flattery

faire elegantly, well
fairnesse leading a good life
falding coarse cloth
famulier well known to
farsed stuffed
faste nearby
fayn gladly
fee simple freehold
felawe companion; rascal
felawschip company; fellowship
felicitee happiness
fer far
ferme annual payment
ferne distant, foreign
ferre, ferrer further
ferreste furthest
ferther further
ferthing a fourth part; a spot;
    a farthing
festne fasten
fetis neat
fetisly neatly, accurately, properly
fetys well made
feyne make up
feyned imitation
fil, fille fell
Finistere Cape Finisterre (N. W.
    Spain)
fissh fish
fithele fiddle
flaterye flattery, lies
Flaundres Flanders
Flaundrish in the style of
    Flanders
flex flax
flok flock
flour flower
flour-de-lys lily
floytinge playing the flute;
    whistling
foo foe

foot-mantel outer skirt used when
    riding
for-pyned wasted away
foreward agreement
forheed forehead
forme propriety
forneys furnace
forster forester
fortunen foretell
forward agreement
fother cart-load
foughten fought
fowel bird
fowles birds
frankeleyn prosperous landowner
fraternitee brotherhood, fraternity,
    guild
fredom integrity
freend friend
freendes friends
Frensh French
fro from
fustian coarse cloth
fyn, fyne fine
fyneste most expensive; best
fyr-reed fiery red
fyve five

gadrede gathered
Galice Galicia (in N. W. Spain,
    famous for shrine of Santiago de
    Compostela)
galingale sweet Cyperus root
gamed pleasant
garleek garlic
gat-tothed gap-toothed
gauded furnished with large beads
Gaunt Ghent
gay showily dressed
gelding gelding, castrated horse
gentil excellent, well born

175

Glossary

gere utensils
gerland garland
Gernade Granada
gerner garner; grain store, granary
ginglen jingle
gipoun tight-fitting vest, doublet
gipser pouch
girdle(es) belt(s)
girles young people of either sex
girt gathered together
glaringe glaring
glas glass, mirror
gobet small portion
goliardeys teller of bawdy jokes
good properly
goon go
goost ghost, spirit
goot goat
Gootland Gotland (in the Baltic)
goune gown
governaunce management
governynge control
grace favour
graunt grant
grece grease
Grete See Mediterranean Sea
gretter larger
greyn corn
grope test, sound out
ground texture
grounded trained, educated
grys expensive grey fur
gyde guide, leader
gynglen jingling
gyse fashion, way

haberdassher a seller of materials or hats
habergeoun coat of mail
halfe half
halle dining hall

halwes shrines
happe circumstance
hardily certainly
hardy brave; rash; sturdy
harlot low-living person
harlotryes obscene things
harneised equipped
haunt skill
havenes places to anchor
heed head
heeld look after
heeng hung
heer hair
heeth natural open space, heath
heigh high
hem them
heng hung
hente obtain; called
herberwe harbour; resting-place
herde cow-herd, shepherd
heres hairs
hethen heathen
hethenesse heathen lands
heve of harre heave off its hinges
hevene heaven
hewe colour, complexion
highte called
him-selven himself
hipes hips
hir their
hire fee
holpen helped
holt wood, grove
holwe hollow
hond wrist
hoolly wholly
hooste host
hoot, hoote hot
hors horse or horses
hosen stockings
hostelrye inn, public house

hostiler publican
hote hotly
houres astronomical hours
householdere head of household
hy sentence high moral
   significance
hyer upper
hyndreste hindmost
hyne farm labourer

ilke same
in good poynt handsome
infect invalid
inspired breathed upon; quickened

janglere loud talker
japes tricks
jay jay
jet fashion, style
jolitee greater comfort; display
juggement ruling
juste joust

kan knew how
keep care
kene sharp
kepe take care
keper head; prior
kept guarded
knarre fellow
knight of the shire member of
   parliament
knobbes boils, lumps

laas cord; lace
lakkede lacked
large freely
late recently, just
latoun pinchbeck, base metal
Latyn Latin
lazar leper

leed cauldron
leet let
lekes leeks
lene lend; skinny
lengthe height
lerned learned
lessoun lesson
lest delight, pleasure
leste if you please
Lettow Lithuania
letuaries electuaries, medicines
lever prefer
lewed unlearned; not in holy orders
leyd laid in
licentiat licensed to hear confession
licour moisture
limitour one who begs within an
   assigned district
list, liste pleased, wished
listes a place for tournaments
litarge white lead
litel little
liveree livery, uniforms
lodemenage piloting
logik philosophy
lokkes locks of hair
lond, of a country, in the
londes lands, countries
looth loath
lordinges my lords
lore law
lough low
love-dayes days fixed for settling
   disputes
love-knotte a complicated twist of
   loops
lowly humble
luce pike (fish)
lust delight
lusty happy, vigorous
lyed lied

Lyeys a place in Armenia (S. W. Turkey)

lyk like

lyned lined

lyte least rich; least important

lyve, lyven live

maad made

magik magic; skills

maister high-placed churchman

maistres masters

maistrye superiority; position of responsibility

make draught

maladye sickness

male bag

maner sort of, type

manere bearing

mantel train

marchant merchant

marshal major-domo, chief steward

martir martyr

mary-bones marrow bones

Maudelayne after St Mary Magdalene

maunciple buyer of provisions for a college or an Inn of Court

Maure Maurus

mayde virgin

mede field

medlee of mixed rich stuff or colour

mercenarie hireling

mere mare

merye happy, jolly

meschief bad times

mesurable moderate

mete food, meat; meal times

mewe coop for fattening birds

millere miller

miscarie come to harm

mister skilled trade

moiste moist

mone moon

moot must, should

mormal open sore, ulcer

morne morning

mortal fatal

mortreux thick soups

morwe morning

morwe-song matins

mottelee a coat of mixed rich stuff or colours

mous mouse

muche great, rich, important

muchel greatly

murierly merrily

mury merry

myrie merry

myrthe happiness

myselven myself

namo no more

narette do not attribute it to

narwe narrow

nas was not

nat not

natheles nevertheless

nedeth needs

neet cattle

nightertale night-time

nones occasion

nonne nun

noon none

noot know not

norissing nourishing

Northfolk Norfolk

nose-thirles nostrils

not-heed closely cropped hair

nought not

nouthe, nowthe now, at this time

ny close

nyce delicate

o one
o-wher anywhere
obstinat stubborn
offring offerings from
   parishioners made voluntarily
offyce secular employment
ofte many
oille of tartre cream of tartar
oistre oyster
oon one
ooth oath
oother other
othes oaths
ounces small portions
oure lady Virgin Mary
out-rydere one who looks after
   outlying areas
outrely outright
overest courtepy outer short cloak
over lippe upper lip
overspradde spread out
owne own
oynement ointment
oynons onions

pace equal; outstrip; pass by
pacient patient
Palatye a place in Anatolia
palfrey riding horse
palmers pilgrims to the Holy Land
pardee by God, indeed
pardoner seller of pardons
pardouns pardons
parfit, parfyt perfect, complete
parisshe parish
parisshens parishioners
partrich partridge
parvys (probably) the portico of
   St Paul's

pas walking pace
patente letters (literally 'open')
   from the king appointing a
   judge
pecok-arwes arrows with peacock's
   feathers used as flights
pees peace
peire a set
penaunce penance
peple people
per-chaunce perhaps
perced pierced
pers bluish-grey
persoun parson
pestilence plague
peyned took pains, endeavoured
phisik, phisyk medicine
Picardye Picardy
pigges pigs
pilwe-beer pillow case
pin brooch
pinche find fault with
pinched pleated
pitaunce a gift (often of food)
pitous full of pity
plentevous plenteous
plesaunt kindly; pleasantly
   behaved
plesen please
pleyen relax
pleyn pure
pleyn by rote recite by heart
pleyn commissioun personal letter
   of appointment as judge
point physical condition
pomely dappled
poraille poor people, 'rubbish'
port bearing
post inn, posting house; support,
   pillar
pouches purses

poudre-marchant sharp flavouring powder

povre poor

poynaunt spicy

poynt nub of the matter

practisour practitioner

preche preach

preest priest

prelat man of the Church

presse curling tongs; mould

pricasour hard rider; a tracker of hares

priketh excites

priking tracking hares

pris price

prively secretly

propre own

proprely faithfully

Pruce Prussia

prys prize; price

pulle pluck, i.e. cheat

pulled plucked

pultrye poultry

purchas profits from begging

purchasour buyer of land

purfiled edged with fur

purs purse

purtreye draw

pylled thin haired

pynnes pins

quik pithy

quik-silver mercury

quyte yow your mede duly reward you

rage indulge in dalliance

Ram the astrological sign of Aries

raughte reach out

rebel rebellious, in disagreement

reckenings, reckenynges bills

recorde recall it to your memory

rede red

reed red; adviser

reherce repeat

rekene calculate

rekening account

relikes relics

remenaunt remainder

renning running

rente income

reportour umpire, judge

resons opinions

resoun reason, reasonable, agreed

reule discipline, rules

reuled governed

reve estate manager

reverence respect

reyn rain

reysed made a military expedition

rood rode

roos rose

roost roast meat

rote fiddle; root

Rouncival Roncesvalles

rouncy common hackney horse

royalliche like a queen

Ruce Russia

rudeliche coarsely

sangwyn blood-red; confident

Satalye a place on the south coast of Asia Minor

saugh saw

sautrye psaltery

savith saveth

sawcefleem afflicted with pimples

sawe saw

scalled scabby

scarsly economically

scathe shame, pity

science knowledge, skills

sclendre slender
scole manner; school
scoler scholar
scoleye study
seche look for
see sea
sege siege
seigh saw
Seint-Jame St James
Seint Julian St Julian
sëynt Loy St Eligius
seke ill, sickly; seek out, visit
seken seek
semely becoming, proper
semi-cope short cloak
sendal rich, thin silk
sentence instruction, learning
sergeant of the lawe senior barrister
servaunts servants
servisable willing to serve
sessiouns meetings of Justices of
   the Peace
sethe seethe, boil
seyl sail
shadwed shaded
shamefastnesse modesty,
   shyness
shapen yow intend, plan
shaply fitted
sheef sheaf
sheeldes crowns (coins)
shene shining
shine shin
shire county, district
shirreve sheriff
shiten dung-covered, dirtied
sho shoe
shoon shone
short little, small
short-sholdred thick-set
shorte shorten

shoures showers
shuldres shoulders
sikerly certainly
sin since
singinge singing
sire president, chairman
slee slay
sleighte trick
smerte unpleasant
smoot smote
smyling smiling
snewed snowed
snibben scold, rebuke
solas amusement
solempne festive; solemn
solempnely pompously
som-del somewhat, rather
somer summer
somnour man who summoned
   people to ecclesiastical courts
sondry various
sonne sun
soong sang
soothly truly
sop piece of cake or bread
soper supper
sort destiny
sote sweet
soun sound
souninge concerning; proclaiming
souple soft and close-fitting
sovereyn highest
sowe sow, pig
sowne sound
space period of time
spak spoke
spanne span, hand's breadth
sparwe sparrow
spores spurs
springe spring, rise
spyced scrupulous

staf staff, stick

statut statute

stemed steamed; **glistened**

stepe bright, fiery

sterres stars

stewe fishpond

stif strong bass voice

stiwardes stewards

stonde be ranked

stonden stand

stoor store cattle, **livestock**

stot cob

straunge foreign, **unknown**

streem stream, **river**

streit strict

strem stream, **river**

stremes currents

strike hank

strondes **shores**

substaunce **money**

subtilly cleverly

suffisaunce contentment

suffre allow

superfluitee excess

surcote long **overcoat**

swerd sword

swere swear

swich such

swink, swinken work, **labour**

swinkere worker

swyn pigs

symple unaffected

sythes times

tabard herald's sleeveless coat; ploughman's loose **smock**

taille credit

take keep

takel equipment

talen to tell tales

tapicer upholsterer

tappestere female publican, barmaid

targe shield

tart sharp

tarynge tarrying, delay

telleth tells

temple Inn of Court

tendre tender, new

termes express in proper form; legal terms

text frequently quoted statement

than then

ther-to in addition

there as where that

thereof of this

thereto moreover

thestat the social position

thikke muscular

thing legal agreement

thombe thumb

thresshe thresh

thries three times

thriftily serviceably

thryes three times

thynne thin

tipet loose hood

toft tuft

togidre together

tollen take payment or toll

Tramissene Tlemcen (N. Algeria)

tretys well shaped

trewe true, honest

trompe trumpet, trumpeter

trouthe integrity

trowe believe

trussed folded up

tukked tucked up round him

Turkye Turkey

tweye two

twinne depart

tydes tides

undergrowe short
undertake take responsibility
untrewe false
usage skills

vavasour country gentleman
venerie hunting
verdit decision; opinion
vernicle a miniature of the face of
    Christ
verrail very
verray truly
vertu vital energy
veyl veil
veyne channel for sap
viage journey
vigilyës celebrations
vileinye unbecoming a gentleman
visage face
vitaille victuals, food
vouche-sauf condescend
voys voice

wandring wandering
wantown wild, lively, loose-living
wantownesse affectation
war aware; let him know of; wary
wastel-breed bread made of the
    best flour
waterlees out of water
wateryng watering place for horses
wayted looked for
webbe male weaver
wel well
wende go
wente walked
weren were
werken make happen, do
werre war, service
werte wart
wex wax

weye wayside
weyeden weighed
whan when
wheither whether
whelkes pimples
whelpe like a puppy
whoso whomsoever
whyl while
whylom once upon a time
whyt, whyte white
widwe widow
wif wife
wight person
wimpel a linen veil covering the
    head, neck and sides of face
winne prove him in arrears
winnyng profits
wiste knew
wit intelligence
with alle moreover
withholde kept in retirement
withouten without
withseye disagree with, contradict
wo in trouble
wode-craft woodcraft, forestry
wolden wished
wonderly wonderfully
wone custom
woning, woninge house, dwelling
    place
wood crazy
woot know
worstede woven cloth
worthy honourable
wrastling wrestling
wrighte craftsman
wroghte did (good deeds)
wrooth angry
wrought made
wryte write
wyd wide

Glossary

wyde large
wyn wine
wynd wind
wynne win
wys, wyse deliberation matter for discussion; prudent, wise, learned

y-bore carried
y-chaped capped
y-come come (past tense)
y-drawe stolen
y-falle fallen
y-go given over to
y-knowe known
y-lad carried
y-lyk like
y-preved proved, tested
y-punisshed punished
y-ronne run
y-shadwed overshadowed
y-shorn cut
y-shrive confessed
y-taught taught

y-teyd tied
y-wimpled covered with wimples, i.e. wearing many veils over her head
y-wroght made
yaf gave
yë eye
yeddinges popular songs
yeeve utensils
yeldhalle guildhall
yelding, yeldynge yield
yeman yeoman, senior servant
yemanly as befits a yeoman
yerde stick, three-foot measure
yeve give
yeven gave
yit yet
yive give
ymages astrological signs or talismans
yow you

Zephirus personification of the West Wind

MORE ABOUT PENGUINS, PELICANS
AND PUFFINS

For further information about books available from Penguins please write to Dept EP, Penguin Books Ltd, Harmondsworth, Middlesex UB7 0DA.

In the U.S.A.: For a complete list of books available from Penguins in the United States write to Dept DG, Penguin Books, 299 Murray Hill Parkway, East Rutherford, New Jersey 07073.

In Canada: For a complete list of books available from Penguins in Canada write to Penguin Books Canada Ltd, 2801 John Street, Markham, Ontario L3R 1B4.

In Australia: For a complete list of books available from Penguins in Australia write to the Marketing Department, Penguin Books Australia Ltd, P.O. Box 257, Ringwood, Victoria 3134.

In New Zealand: For a complete list of books available from Penguins in New Zealand write to the Marketing Department, Penguin Books (N.Z.) Ltd, Private Bag, Takapuna, Auckland 9.

In India: For a complete list of books available from Penguins in India write to Penguin Overseas Ltd, 706 Eros Apartments, 56 Nehru Place, New Delhi 110019.

Penguin Masterstudies

Already published:

Subjects

Applied Mathematics
Biology
Geography
Pure Mathematics

Literature

The Mill on the Floss
Persuasion
Vanity Fair
The Wasteland

Chaucer

The Miller's Tale
The Nun's Priest's Tale
The Prologue to The Canterbury Tales

Shakespeare

Hamlet
Othello
A Shakespeare Handbook

Penguin Classics

CHAUCER

Translated by Nevill Coghill

TROILUS AND CRISEYDE

During the great siege of Troy, quizzing the girls in the temple, Troilus sees Criseyde and falls in love with her. Later, with the help of Pandarus, the first great comic character of English literature, Troilus wins Criseyde's love and this is the beginning of his joy, just as later it is to cause his sorrow and death.

Troilus and Criseyde (*c.* 1380 85) is both comedy and tragedy. Nevill Coghill counts himself among those who believe it to be the most beautiful long poem in the English language. In it Chaucer 'meditates on the nature of love as it enraptures and afflicts us in this sublunary world'.

THE CANTERBURY TALES

The Canterbury Tales stands conspicuous among the great literary achievements of the Middle Ages. Told by a jovial procession of pilgrims knight, priest, yeoman, miller, or cook as they ride towards the shrine of Thomas à Becket, they present a picture of a nation taking shape. The tone of this never-resting comedy is, by turns, learned, fantastic, lewd, pious, and ludicrous. 'Here', as John Dryden said, 'is God's plenty!'

Geoffrey Chaucer began his great task in about 1386. This version in modern English, by Nevill Coghill, preserves the freshness and racy vitality of Chaucer's narrative.

New Penguin Shakespeare
GENERAL EDITOR: T. J. B. SPENCER

ENGLISH AND
AMERICAN LITERATURE

☐ *Helbeck of Bannisdale* **Mrs Humphrey Ward**   £3.50

Edited by Brian Worthington. Written in 1898, a classic to rate with
the novels of George Eliot and Charlotte Brontë, this is a subtle and
impressive treatment of 'the love between man and woman'.

☐ *The Red Badge of Courage* **Stephen Crane**   £1.50

Introduced by Pascal Covici, Jr. 'A psychological portrayal of fear',
and one of the greatest novels ever written about war: the story of a
raw Union recruit during the American Civil War.

☐ *Heart of Darkness* **Joseph Conrad**   £0.95

Conrad's most profound exploration of human savagery and de-
spair is contained in this story of Marlowe's search for Mister Kurtz in
the jungle of the Belgian Congo: a vision that has haunted readers,
novelists and poets throughout the century.

☐ *Selected Writings* **Samuel Johnson**   £3.95

Edited by Patrick Cruttwell. Including generous selections from his
Dictionary, his edition of Shakespeare, and his *Lives of the Poets*,
plus excerpts from his journalism, letters and private prayers.

☐ *Call It Sleep* **Henry Roth**   £3.50

Published in 1934, this extraordinary novel reveals, through the eyes
of David Schearl (the son of immigrant Jews), a profusion of life and
family relationships in the teeming jungle of a New York City slum.

☐ *A Journey to the Western Islands of Scotland*
Johnson
The Journal of a Tour to the Hebrides **Boswell**   £3.50

Edited by Peter Levi. These two journals of their joint tour of
Scotland in 1773 are masterpieces of travel-writing, human observation and glorious, sardonic wit.

ENGLISH AND
AMERICAN LITERATURE

☐ *The House in Paris* **Elizabeth Bowen** £2.50

A novel that crystallizes, with delicacy and wit, the disturbing relationships between children, sex and love. 'All Miss Bowen's most brilliant qualities are here' – Jocelyn Brooke

☐ *Look Homeward, Angel* **Thomas Wolfe** £4.95

A young boy grows to manhood in small-town America. Here Wolfe displays, said F. Scott Fitzgerald, 'that flair for the extravagant and fantastic which has been an American characteristic from Irving and Poe to Dashiell Hammett'.

☐ *The Aspern Papers* and *The Turn of the Screw*
Henry James £1.95

Edited by Anthony Curtis. Containing James's two most dramatic and masterly tales: the first, a story of literary 'spoils and stratagems' set in Venice; the last, a ghost story that still puzzles the critics and terrifies all its readers.

☐ *Martin Eden* **Jack London** £2.95

Based on the author's own turbulent and legendary life, the story of a young San Franciscan seaman and his struggle to win intellectual and social recognition.

☐ *The Enlarged Devil's Dictionary* **Ambrose Bierce** £3.95

Edited by Ernest Jerome Hopkins. Containing 1,851 definitions, this spicy, satirical dictionary is for all those 'who prefer dry wines to sweet, sense to sentiment, wit to humour . . .'

☐ *The Unfortunate Traveller and Other Works*
Thomas Nashe £2.95

Edited by J. B. Steane. Sketches and writings by one of Shakespeare's most lively contemporaries: the journalist, storyteller, irreverent social critic, jester and entertainer who epitomizes the flavour and bawdy vitality of the Elizabethans.

ENGLISH AND
AMERICAN LITERATURE

☐ *News from Nowhere* **William Morris** £2.95

Edited by Asa Briggs. The Utopian novel, plus a selection of designs, letters, verse and writings by this brilliant artist and most unorthodox Victorian.

☐ *Barchester Towers* **Anthony Trollope** £1.95

Edited by Robin Gilmour. Trollope's most popular novel, and a superb comic portrayal of life and society in mid-Victorian England.

These books should be available at all good bookshops or newsagents, but if you live in the UK or the Republic of Ireland and have difficulty in getting to a bookshop, they can be ordered by post. Please indicate the titles required and fill in the form below.

NAME _____ BLOCK CAPITALS

ADDRESS _____

_____

_____

Enclose a cheque or postal order payable to The Penguin Bookshop to cover the total price of books ordered, plus 50p for postage. Readers in the Republic of Ireland should send £IR equivalent to the sterling prices, plus 67p for postage. Send to: The Penguin Bookshop, 54/56 Bridlesmith Gate, Nottingham, NG1 2GP.

You can also order by phoning (0602) 599295, and quoting your Barclaycard or Access number.

Every effort is made to ensure the accuracy of the price and availability of books at the time of going to press, but it is sometimes necessary to increase prices and in these circumstances retail prices may be shown on the covers of books which may differ from the prices shown in this list or elsewhere. This list is not an offer to supply any book.

This order service is only available to residents in the UK and the Republic of Ireland.